Dad,   20 May 2001

Happy Birthday.

Charlie

Happy Birthday

Portrait of
AUSTRALIA

Portrait of
AUSTRALIA
ROBIN SMITH

NEW
HOLLAND

For Alison, Hugh, Louise, Victoria, Virginia, Susan, James and Richard

Contents

ARAFURA
SEA

MELVILLE
ISLAND

TIMOR
SEA

DARWIN ○

ARNHEM
LAND

Katherine

INDIAN
OCEAN

Wyndham

KIMBERLEY
REGION

Tanami
Desert

Broome

Tennant
Creek

NORTHERN
TERRITORY

HAMERSLEY RANGE

Newman

GIBSON
DESERT

MACDONNELL RANGE

Alice
Spring

Uluru ○

Carnarvon ○

LITTLE SANDY DESERT

TROPIC OF
CAPRICORN

WESTERN
AUSTRALIA

SOUTH
AUSTRALIA

GREAT VICTORIA
DESERT

Coo
P

NULLARBOR PLAIN

Kalgoorlie ○

PERTH ○
Fremantle

DARLING RANGE

GREAT AUSTRALIAN
BIGHT

SOUTHERN
OCEAN

THURSDAY
ISLAND

GREAT BARRIER REEF

CORAL
SEA

GULF OF
CARPENTARIA

CAPE
YORK
PENINSULA

Cooktown

Cairns

SOUTH
PACIFIC
OCEAN

GREAT

Townsville

WHITSUNDAY
ISLANDS

Mount
Isa

DIVIDING

Longreach

Rockhampton

QUEENSLAND

RANGE

MPSON
DESERT

STURT STONY
DESERT

Lake Eyre

BRISBANE
Gold Coast

STRZELECKI
DESERT

Lake
Torrens

Lake
Frome

Darling River

NEW
SOUTH WALES

Port
Augusta

Broken
Hill

Bathurst

N

Port
Lincoln

Murray River

Newcastle

0   200   400km

DELAIDE

SYDNEY

ACT

CANBERRA

ANGAROO
ISLAND

VICTORIA

MELBOURNE

FLINDERS
ISLAND

Launceston

TASMANIA

HOBART

TASMAN
SEA

Introduction

Australia is one of the most extraordinary countries on earth. Its sprawling landscape—more than 3000 million years in the making—ranges from dense tropical rainforest and arid, sandy desert to lush riverland and golden, surf-fringed beaches. This vast and geographically diverse continent—the driest on earth—extends 4025 kilometres from east to west and passes through three time zones. Girdled by the Tropic of Capricorn, it stretches 3700 kilometres from the sweltering north to the temperate south.

With a landmass of 7 692 030 square kilometres, Australia is the world's largest island and the sixth largest country on earth. It dwarfs Western Europe in size, yet its population is a mere 19 million—little more than the Netherlands. Australia's indigenous population are the Aboriginal people, who have roamed the continent for many thousands of years and have a rich and vibrant culture based on a spiritual association with the land. Without a written history, Aboriginal culture and stories of the Dreamtime have been passed down from generation to generation through music, rock drawings and paintings.

European settlement began in the late 18th century, after navigator Captain James Cook saw the land's potential when he sailed along the east coast in 1770. Britain soon recognised the disadvantages of Australia's distance and isolation as a solution to its overcrowded prisons, and on 26 January 1788, a day still celebrated as 'Australia Day', Captain Arthur Phillip sailed into Sydney Harbour to establish the country's first convict colony. After eight months at sea, the convicts, soldiers and free citizens on the First Fleet of 11 ships stepped ashore to an uncertain future, struggling to create a settlement in isolated and harsh conditions.

Today, Australia is a federation of six states and two territories, which were originally established as separate British colonies. On 1 January 1901, the disparate colonies were united as the Commonwealth of Australia, with each state retaining certain autonomous powers. It is this inherent sense of both unity and independence that pervades the Australian character.

The harsh terrain of the country's interior wilderness has prompted the majority of the population to live in urban centres along the east coast. Australia's cities are melting pots

ABOVE: The Northern Territory's Desert Park is home to a selection of the many species of wildflowers that bloom across the desert.

OPPOSITE: In Kalbarri National Park, Western Australia, breathtaking ochre coastal cliffs frame the deep blues of sea and sky.

of hedonistic beach culture, a thriving business and cultural life, and a cosmopolitanism derived from the waves of European and Asian migration during the 20th century. Urban communities reflect immigrant cultures from more than 150 nationalities, each of whom has brought the traditions of their homeland to this land of opportunity, where they embrace change, unfamiliar customs, unexplored vistas, even reversed seasons, to make new lives for themselves and their families.

Australians make the most of their 17 700 kilometres of coastline, which ranges from wind-scarred cliffs and icy ocean-breakers to sultry seashores and azure waters. The Australian dedication to water sports—swimming, surfing, fishing and boating—is world-renowned, and virtually all the major cities are built on the shores of a harbour, or within easy reach of the coast. Most of Australia's inland, however, is barren and at the mercy of extreme weather conditions. Sprawling Outback cattle stations, some the size of small European countries, exist at the ends of dirt tracks amid the ever-present dust. The tyranny of distance and the weather-dominated landscape dictate the interior's isolated lifestyle and the unreliable rural economy.

This diverse and spectacular island continent is home to an amazing range of unique wildlife, from egg-laying mammals to ancient reptiles and pouched marsupials. The country's flora is equally distinctive: the Australian gum tree is recognised throughout the world as characteristic of the landscape, and vast mountain ranges are hazed in blue-green from the oily leaves of more than 600 varieties of eucalypts. These hardy green trees are susceptible to fire and the country can be ravaged by ferocious bushfires during the hot dry summers.

Australia, the great southern land, embraces diversity in its contrasting landscapes, multi-cultural population and unique wildlife. It is a nation that pulsates to the beat of ancient rhythms as well as the vitality of modern civilisation.

LEFT: Dramatic vistas and magnificent natural beauty are characteristics of Australia. Here, the Sydney Harbour Bridge, an icon of Australia, is silhouetted against the backdrop of a stunning fiery cloudscape.

ABOVE: Australia boasts several islands that rise dramatically from the ocean. Lord Howe Island, north-east of Sydney, is home to dense vegetation, a coral reef and even a blue lagoon. Its population is about 200.

LEFT: Australians are obsessed with fishing—in rivers, creeks and dams as well as the ocean. Rock fishing is classified as Australia's most dangerous sport, due to the frightening risk of being swept away by a sudden wave.

BELOW LEFT: The surf lifesaving movement is both an essential and a recreational component of the Australian lifestyle. Surf lifesavers perform many rescues each year on Australia's beaches, but they also find time for carnivals.

BELOW RIGHT: Kangaroo Island, off the coast of South Australia, is renowned as a paradise for animal lovers and birdwatchers. Pelicans are found both inland, in lagoons and rivers, as well as on the coast.

ABOVE: In the heart of the Australian bush, a group of stockmen break for 'smoko' around their campfire. Quintessentially Australian scenes such as this are the subject of many well-known paintings, by artists such as Frederick McCubbin and Arthur Streeton.

RIGHT: With his rolled-up shirt sleeves, Akubra and weather-beaten, sun-baked face, Bill Hayes is typical of the hardy men who live and work on the cattle stations of the Outback.

BELOW RIGHT: Australia's indigenous Aboriginal people have a rich tradition of painting and drawing episodes from the stories of the Dreamtime. Bark painting, using bark from the Stringy-bark tree, is one of the world's oldest continuing artistic traditions.

ABOVE: The small township of Bright, in Victoria, is well-known for its avenues of deciduous trees, which provide welcome shade in summer, and a beautiful show of colour during autumn.

LEFT: Queensland's Norman River winds its way northward to the Gulf of Carpentaria. During the wet season, when heavy rains fall for days on end, the river swells and turns the surrounding plains into an inland sea.

ABOVE LEFT: The Koala is one of the most well-known and loved Australian animals. Its diet consists of mildly-toxic eucalypt leaves, which cause Koalas to sleep for up to 19 hours a day.

ABOVE RIGHT: The Stirling Ranges, in Western Australia, are home to many varieties of wildflowers.

BELOW LEFT: The highly distinctive and flamboyant colours of the Crimson Rosella make it one of the most beautiful Australian birds. It lives on fruit and seeds, and nests in tree hollows.

BELOW MIDDLE: The Bottlebrush is a familiar native Australian plant. It thrives in hot, dry conditions.

BELOW RIGHT: The Tasmanian Devil, so named for its 'devilish' appearance, is the world's largest surviving carnivorous marsupial, and is only found in Tasmania.

QUEENSLAND

Tweed Heads

Lismore
Casino
Tenterfield   Ballina

Lightning Ridge   Moree   **38**   1

STURT
N.P.
Tibooburra

Bourke

Darling River

71

White
Cliffs

MOOTWINGEE
N.P.

MITCHELL HWY

Armidale   DORRIGO
N.P.

NEW ENGLAND HWY   Coffs
Harbour

55

34

Coonabarabran   Tamworth

BARRINGTON
TOPS N.P.   Port
Macquarie

Broken Hill

SOUTH AUSTRALIA

Menindee

NEW
SOUTH
WALES

Dubbo   **15**

HUNTER VALLEY   PACIFIC HWY

MUNGO
N.P.   Parkes

32

Cessnock   MYALL LAKES
N.P.

79

39

Orange   Bathurst
32   Lithgow

Newcastle

WOLLEMI
N.P.

Wentworth

24

Cowra

BLUE
MOUNTAINS N.P.
Parramatta   SYDNEY

SOUTH
PACIFIC
OCEAN

Murray River

20

75

41

Wollongong

Goulburn   **31**

Gundagai
Wagga
Wagga   **20**

MORTON
N.P.

Tumut   CANBERRA   Nowra

N

Hume Hwy   A.C.T.
18

Albury   KOSCIUSZKO
N.P.
Thredbo

Cooma   **0   100   200km**

VICTORIA   **23**   Bega   1

Eden

TASMAN
SEA

BEN BOYD N.P.

New South Wales

New South Wales, the nation's first state, epitomises all that is Australian—from its progressive cities and sandy surf beaches, to its Outback wilderness.

The first and largest city in Australia is Sydney, with the famous sparkling harbour at its heart—a network of gentle waterways and playground for the four million residents who call Sydney home. With its world-renowned twin icons of the Sydney Opera House and Harbour Bridge, and a magnificent coastline of bays, inlets and beaches, Sydney undoubtedly has one of the most beautiful harbours in the world. Passenger ferries criss-cross the water, gliding alongside luxurious passenger liners and yachts catching the breeze. Sydney's coastal suburbs are fringed by an endless horizon of ocean surf stretching as far as Palm Beach in the north, and encompassing the famous Bondi in the east. The popular suburb of Manly, a half-hour ferry ride from the city, offers sheltered harbour beaches on the west side and golden surf beaches on the east.

Today's glamorous city had its beginnings in 1788 when Sydney was chosen as a bleak convict outpost, with little to sustain the early settlers except a grim determination to survive and a dream of freedom. An echo of those primitive days still exists at the Rocks, where historic buildings are accessible among a maze of cobblestone lanes and old pubs. Other early buildings include New South Wales Parliament House, the Mitchell Library and Hyde Park Barracks, all in Macquarie Street. Through the spacious gardens of the Domain is the Art Gallery of New South Wales which has one of the finest collections in the country, and, opposite Hyde Park, the Australian Museum, regarded as one of the best natural history museums in the world.

To the west, at Sydney's geographic centre, is Homebush Bay, site of the 2000 Olympic Games. The Olympic stadium, aquatic centre and Olympic village, among other ultra-modern sporting facilities, are here. Nearby Parramatta is the site of the country's first land grant where Old Government House still stands—Australia's oldest public building.

Heading west from Sydney, the hazy Blue Mountains offer panoramic views of rocky outcrops, cascading waterfalls and rugged terrain that were an early barrier to exploration of the

ABOVE: Near Khancoban, at the outlet of the Murray One Power Station which forms part of the Snowy Mountains Hydro-electric Scheme, is a pondage which is not only scenic but a popular place for fishing and picnics. The released water, together with the Swampy Plain River, joins the Murray River a short distance downstream.

state's inland to the west. The mountains were traversed in 1813 by Wentworth, Blaxland and Lawson, opening up access to the fertile plains and mining areas of the interior.

Australia's second oldest city, not far north of Sydney, is the coal-mining centre of Newcastle. Nearby, the fertile Hunter Valley is renowned for its wineries, and beyond lie rugged bushlands and vast sheep and cattle studs. Heading north, the Pacific Highway meanders parallel to the eastern coastline of surf beaches. Australia's casual beach culture and relaxed lifestyle is evident at towns along the coast, such as Port Macquarie, Coffs Harbour and the continent's most easterly point, Byron Bay.

South of Sydney lie the bush-clad gullies and escarpments behind the industrial centre of Wollongong, and the coastal towns and beaches of the Sapphire Coast. Inland, the rural countryside of the picturesque Southern Highlands shelters charming historic villages that reflect the way of life of bygone days. Way out west, the Outback mining centre of Broken Hill and other once prosperous ghost towns, recall the gold rushes of over 100 years ago.

Beyond the Great Dividing Range is the scenic New England region and the university city of Armidale where seasons are clearly defined and the hills and valleys are reminiscent of the English countryside. The mountainous, harsh terrain of the south-west becomes the Snowy Mountains National Park and an alpine playground. Mount Kosciuszko is a magnet to skiers and snowboarders, as well as bush walkers in the warmer months.

Geographically diverse and historically fascinating, New South Wales is a forward-moving, dynamic state, and a micro-cosom of all that is recognisably Australian.

LEFT: Magnificent Sydney Harbour is the jewel in Australia's crown, and the showpiece of a nation. The city itself, located on the shores of this vast body of water, has long been acclaimed as one of the world's most beautiful. Thriving and modern, Sydney today would be unrecognisable to the convicts and sailors who first landed at Sydney Cove on 26 January 1788.

ABOVE: Commanding attention from all directions across the harbour, Sydney's two masterpieces of 20th century architecture stand like sentinels on either side of Sydney Cove. For many people, the vast arch of the Harbour Bridge and the glistening, white sails of the Opera House are twin symbols of Australia, and a spectacular sight by day or night.

RIGHT: With its crenellated battlement, turrets and magnificent interiors, Government House, built between 1837 and 1845, is a sophisticated example of Gothic Revival architecture. The outstanding collections of 19th and 20th century furnishings and decorations, on display in the State Rooms, reflect the differing tastes of successive Governors–General who have lived here.

ABOVE: On New Year's Eve the Harbour becomes the stage for Sydney's boisterous celebrations. Throughout the night, Sydneysiders gather along the surrounding foreshores and, on the stroke of midnight, a breathtaking display of fireworks explodes from the Harbour Bridge, illuminating the night sky and heralding the New Year with awesome spectacle.

FAR LEFT: Darling Harbour is the playground of Sydney Harbour, a popular area of cafés, restaurants, hotels and convention centres, shopping malls and entertainment zones. Throughout the year, Darling Harbour plays host to various festivals and celebrations, including fireworks and laser displays.

LEFT: A far cry from the busy cafés and social spots of Darling Harbour is the Chinese Garden of Friendship. Donated in 1988 by the Guangdong Province of China, the garden is a fine example of Chinese landscaping. Behind its sheltering walls are peaceful gardens and waterfalls, much beloved as a quiet retreat by Sydneysiders.

RIGHT: The Rocks, Sydney's oldest area, nestles in the shadow of the Harbour Bridge and still preserves its authentic atmosphere despite undergoing many changes over the years. Its biggest facelift occurred during the 1920s, when the construction of the Harbour Bridge necessitated the removal of three streets and changed the skyline forever.

BELOW: On the edge of Sydney Harbour, the city's Royal Botanic Gardens are home to an extensive collection of plants from Australia and overseas. Located in the gardens is the Choragic Monument of Lysicrates, a scaled down Victorian replica of the original which was erected in Athens in 334 BC.

ABOVE: Anzac Bridge was known for some years as the Glebe Island Bridge, but was renamed in 1999 in honour of the Anzacs—the Australia and New Zealand Army Corps—who fought in the two world wars of the 20th century. The main span of the concrete bridge is 345 metres long.

RIGHT: At a height of some 300 metres above the city, the AMP Tower, thrusting above the Centrepoint Arcade, is a prominent landmark and a distinctive feature of the Sydney cityscape. To mark Sydney's status as an Olympic host, three statues of athletes crown the rim. On a clear day, the views from the tower across the city to the Blue Mountains in the distance are spectacular.

FAR RIGHT: Vaucluse House, an elegant, sandstone mansion with Gothic turrets and castellations, was home to the Wentworth family from 1827 to 1853. Set in 27 acres of beautiful grounds, the house has been preserved to give an insight into life in colonial Sydney.

BELOW: Every year on Boxing Day, a fleet of yachts leave Sydney Harbour on the start of a 630 nautical mile journey to Hobart in Tasmania. The Sydney–Hobart Yacht Race has been in existence for over 50 years and is one of the world's great blue water classics.

ABOVE LEFT: An unusual landmark of Kings Cross is the El Alamein fountain, designed by Robert Woodward in 1961 to commemorate the El Alamein battle of World War II. Consisting of 211 stalks attached to a spherical spray, the fountain has been copied around the world.

ABOVE RIGHT: Characterised by its elegant 19th century terraced houses, with their iron lace balconies, the eastern suburb of Paddington is one of the most prestigious and picturesque areas of inner city Sydney. Discreetly gentrified, Paddington is a cultural microcosm of Sydney with a fascinating assortment of old façades, ultra-modern interiors, high-quality antique shops and turn-of-the-century pubs.

LEFT: Once described as the finest house in the colony, Elizabeth Bay House is indeed a superb example of colonial architecture, with magnificent views over Sydney Harbour. Among its many distinguishing features is the impressive stone staircase, which sweeps out from an elliptical, domed hall. The quality of workmanship in the joinery, stonework and plasterwork has rarely been equalled in Australia.

ABOVE LEFT: Most visitors to Australia make a beeline for Uluru, Sydney Harbour...and Bondi Beach. Renowned throughout the world as the epitome of Australian beach culture, the sweeping bay with its background of apartment blocks and cafés is an impressive sight on a hot summer's day, when barely an inch of sand is left vacant. The surf-reel, Australia's first surf lifesaving device, was invented at Bondi.

ABOVE RIGHT: Besides achieving fame as the beach that rejected the popular television series *Baywatch*, Avalon Beach is also known as one of Sydney's cleanest. The surf here is excellent, and swimming and fishing are also popular recreational activities.

BELOW: In the early 1900s, when sea bathing was a new venture, the first surf lifesaving clubs were formed in response to the many drownings that occurred. Although rubber dinghies are now used as rescue vehicles, the traditional wooden rowing boats are still used for competitions against other clubs.

OPPOSITE: At the northern end of Sydney's Northern Beaches, a 15-kilometre long promontory known as the 'Peninsula' is home to some of the most prestigious and expensive real estate in Sydney. On the east side, scenic beaches offer good surf, while on the west side the tranquil waterway of Pittwater is home to yachts of all sizes. Dominating Barrenjoey Head, at Sydney's northernmost point, is an 1881 lighthouse, a prominent landmark which affords fabulous views.

ABOVE: At Homebush Bay, to the west of the city, a complex of state-of-the-art stadia and sports centres has risen from land that was formerly swamp. Host to the 2000 Olympic Games, the area comprises the most modern sports facilities in the world. Among these is the Sydney International Aquatic Centre, completed in 1994, and the scene of many medal-winning swims. Besides the Olympic pool, the Centre also includes a training pool and family fun pool.

OPPOSITE TOP AND BOTTOM: The showpiece of the Olympic site is Stadium Australia, central venue of the 2000 Olympic Games. As the largest outdoor venue in Olympic history, the building is suitably impressive, with seating for 110 000 cleverly designed to provide maximum shelter from the harsh Australian climate. As the venue for the Opening and Closing ceremonies of the Olympics, the A$690 million stadium has become the third world-famous icon of Sydney.

ABOVE: The town of Parramatta, Australia's second oldest settlement, grew up around Government House, a fine, Georgian building, which served as a vice-regal country retreat, and was built between 1790 and 1816.

RIGHT: The diversity of flora in the gardens of Mount Wilson makes it one of the most beautiful villages in the Blue Mountains. Visitors flock to see the colourful displays in spring and autumn.

BELOW: The charming town of Windsor on the Hawkesbury River, laid out by Governor Macquarie in 1810, preserves many historic buildings. Chief among these is St Matthews Anglican Church, designed by convict architect Francis Greenway, and considered by many to be his finest work.

TOP: From the Kanangra Walls, the Blue Mountains National Park stretches to the horizon in a breathtaking display of gullies and eucalypt forests. Part of the Great Dividing Range, the area takes its name from the blue mist that rises from thousands of eucalyptus trees and mingles with the mountain air, tinting both sky and mountains with an unmistakable blue hue.

LEFT AND ABOVE: Controversial artist and poet Norman Lindsay spent 60 years of his life in a house he called Olympia, at Springwood in the Blue Mountains. Here, Lindsay painted his famous nudes, that were considered scandalous in their day, and created his much loved children's book, *The Magic Pudding*. Today, the house and studio have been preserved by the National Trust, providing a fascinating glimpse into Lindsay's bohemian lifestyle and showcasing some of his finest works.

RIGHT: Perhaps the most famous landmark of the Blue Mountains is the geological formation known as the Three Sisters. According to Aboriginal legend, these gnarled, rocky points are three beautiful young sisters who were turned to stone by their father in order to prevent them being carried off by an enemy. The father was killed before the spell could be reversed, and the sisters remain for eternity overlooking some of the most magnificent vistas imaginable.

ABOVE: The thunderous surf of Avoca Beach makes this secluded spot a popular holiday resort and favourite destination among surfing fanatics. The area is the traditional home of the Awabakal Aboriginal people but has been occupied by Europeans since 1830.

LEFT: Putty Beach at Box Head forms part of Bouddi National Park, and is one of several small, secluded beaches that guard the untouched bush of the hinterland. The name Bouddi is Aboriginal for 'water breaking over rocks'.

ABOVE AND RIGHT: A place synonymous in Australia with fine wine is the Hunter Valley. Based around the old country town of Cessnock, the Hunter area has been planted with vines for over 150 years. The landscape is overwhelmingly rural—green farming pastures are interspersed with vineyards producing wines that have won many national and international awards.

BELOW: The wine country of the Hunter Valley offers many diversions to visitors, including winery tours and ballooning, and as such it is a popular weekend escape hatch from the big cities along the coast. Hotels such as Peppers Guest House, nestled in the heart of the Hunter Valley, provide good food, fine wine and peaceful gardens in which to stroll.

LEFT: The large industrial and port city of Newcastle thrives on the coal which is mined in the upper Hunter Valley, from where it is transported to Newcastle and exported around the world. Founded in 1804, Newcastle is an attractively located city, with riverside gardens and stately buildings, an indication of the prosperity brought to the city by the discovery of coal in the 19th century.

ABOVE: Myall Lakes National Park, on the central coast of New South Wales, encompasses the largest system of freshwater lakes in the state. The largest of these lagoons, Myall Lake, is 16 kilometres long, and reaches from the hills into a vast stretch of water known as the Broadwater. Tranquil and picturesque, the area is popular with holidaymakers.

LEFT: Byron Bay, the most easterly point of the Australian mainland, is renowned for its spectacular coastline. A popular walk along the clifftop leads to the 1901 lighthouse, once a vital tool for navigation and the most powerful light on the New South Wales coast.

OPPOSITE: About half-way along the Waterfall Way, linking Armidale on the New England tableland with Urunga on the eastern seaboard, is the village of Ebor. At this same point, the Guy Fawkes River drops over a rock escarpment into a deep ravine, becoming the beautiful Ebor Falls.

RIGHT: The gleaming, white temple-like building in the centre of Woolgoolga seems at first a surprising structure for a small Australian coastal town. It is in fact a restaurant, the Raj Mahal, which was built here in response to the large community of Sikhs who live in the town. Many of their ancestors arrived from the Punjab in the late 19th century to work in the canefields of Queensland.

BELOW: At 1157 metres above sea level, Mount Warning, once part of a volcano, towers over the Tweed Valley below. Named in 1770 by Captain Cook, who was almost shipwrecked off the coast, Mount Warning receives the first rays of the rising sun each morning, making it a popular destination at dawn on New Year's Day.

THIS PAGE: Deeargee Station, originally called Gostwyck, was one of the earliest sheep stations established in the New England area. Its most interesting feature is the tiered, octagonal woolshed, which was far ahead of its day when it was built in 1851. The design features a clerestory of glass ventilators which allow light and air for the 24 shearers sweating away below. Merino sheep are still bred and shorn at Deeargee, producing the soft, fine wool that is much prized in Australia and overseas.

ABOVE: In order to protect livestock from attacks by Dingos, Australia's wild dogs, a 5000-kilometre fence was built to keep them out of eastern Australia. The fence, which is nearly two metres high and extends 30 centimetres underground, requires regular maintenance from roving teams of rangers.

RIGHT: Tibooburra, said to be the hottest place in New South Wales, is also the most isolated. It owes its existence to an 1880s gold strike, which saw an influx of 1000 prospecters, and the establishment of the post office and Family Hotel. The murals in the bar were painted in 1970 by three-times Archibald Prize winner, Clifton Pugh.

ABOVE LEFT: Few buildings remain in the ghost town of Silverton, which, for a decade during the 1880s, was a booming silver town, with ten hotels and a brewery. When the riches of Broken Hill were discovered, the prospectors deserted Silverton, taking many of the better houses with them.

ABOVE RIGHT: The town of White Cliffs, in the state's far west, is named after the sole outcrop in which opals are found. The commercial opal fields here are Australia's oldest, and the town supported a population of 5000 during the boom days of the early 20th century.

BELOW LEFT: The main occupation in the Outback town of Broken Hill is mining, but the inhabitants find time to demonstrate their skills at horsemanship. Festivals and rodeos are a popular recreational activity.

BELOW RIGHT: Few Australian goldfields made more fortunes than those around the village of Hill End. Only a small community now remains in the old wooden houses, but several shops, such as the Post Office and St Paul's Presbyterian Church, have been restored.

ABOVE LEFT AND BELOW: Tandou Farm, at Menindee on the banks of the Darling River, is a huge agricultural development. In 1972, a lake was drained to prepare a 13 500 hectare alluvial bed for crops, with irrigation when water is available. Cotton, wheat, barley and various fruits are among the crops successfully grown here. Helicopters are used to herd corellas away from the sunflower crops.

ABOVE RIGHT: One of the members of the Burke and Wills expedition to the Gulf of Carpentaria was Dost Mahomet, an Afghan camel driver. The group passed through the small town of Menindee, and Mahomet later settled there. His grave is located on the outskirts of town.

OPPOSITE: Siding Spring Observatory, established in Warrumbungle National Park in 1974, is one of the world's major astronomical sites. It houses a selection of the world's major telescopes, including Australia's largest—the 3.9 metre Anglo–Australian Telescope.

ABOVE: The Hume Highway meanders through sunburnt landscapes, such as the farmlands near Gundagai. There is no place in Australia more acclaimed in song and verse than this historic town, and by the side of the Hume Highway at Five Mile Creek, passers-by will find the statue of the Dog on the Tuckerbox, whose story is part of Australian folklore.

RIGHT: The town of Tumut, in the foothills of the Snowy Mountains, is famed for the beauty of its trees during autumn. Poplars, Elms, Oaks and Maples line the streets and the town's park, flaming with colour.

ABOVE: The peaceful landscape around Cowra is carpeted by the distinctive purple of the weed known as Patterson's Curse. Its name derives from its invasive spread across farmland, but the weed is also known as Salvation Jane, a reference to the fact that in times of drought the plant does not wither, but provides food for cattle.

LEFT: The old village of Carcoar, in the Central West, retains much of its 19th century charm. Among several old buildings is St Paul's Anglican Church, designed by Edmund Blackett and completed in 1848. The town was also the scene of Australia's first bank hold-up, which took place at the Commercial Bank in 1863.

ABOVE: Situated at the head of the Upper Murrumbidgee River, Tantangara Reservoir forms part of the Snowy Mountains Hydro-electric Scheme and acts as a backup to the major water storage of Lake Eucumbene. The picturesque southern shoreline lies within Kosciuszko National Park.

Thredbo is the most popular, the most expensive and arguably the best of Australia's skiing resorts. Sloping down one side of a steep valley, the resort village is compact and attractive, with Alpine lodges sheltering against the mountains. The air is distinctly European, reminiscent of an Austrian mountain village. The ski runs are on the opposite side of the valley, across the Crackenback River, and chairlifts take skiers to the top of the runs.

ABOVE: Ben Boyd National Park features some outstanding coastal scenery, with sea caves hidden in the rugged cliffs and hills covered with flowering heaths. The park was named after businessman Ben Boyd, who established a whaling station here in 1842, the remains of which can still be visited today.

RIGHT: As its name might suggest, the port town of Eden is built on a bay and coastline of exceptional beauty. The town centre itself sits atop a peninsula, overlooking Snug Cove which harbours a large fishing fleet. Eden was established in 1818 as the first whaling station on the Australian mainland, an industry which continued here until the 1920s.

LEFT: The blue–grey basalt rocks south of Narooma are known as the Glasshouse Rocks, so-called for their glass-like appearance when they glisten in sun and rain. Their existence is the result of volcanic activity around Mount Dromedary eons ago.

BELOW: In the 1840s, Ben Boyd envisaged a town to rival the main port of Eden, which he planned to build across the bay and would name Boydtown. However, his ideas proved to be too grandiose and his ambitious plans were never realised, save for a few buildings which today stand in ruins, the symbol of a broken dream.

ABOVE: Goulburn, the second oldest city in inland Australia, is the centre of a prosperous farming region known as the Southern Tablelands. For over 150 years, the fertile plains of the area have been renowned for their produce, ranging from wool at Goulburn to potatoes at nearby Crookwell.

RIGHT: The area known as the Southern Highlands, near Wollongong, is a place of rural peace and has an agreeable climate. In the pretty town of Bowral, popular since the 19th century as a fashionable resort among Sydney's wealthy families, a Tulip Festival is held annually which draws large crowds.

BELOW: Australia's seventh largest city, Wollongong, is situated along a shoreline of beaches at the foot of the Illawarra Plateau. Settlers arrived here in 1815, and since then the city has grown into an urbanised area, stretching 15 kilometres along the coast. Heavy industry predominates, including the country's largest steel works.

ABOVE: The Waratah is the floral emblem of New South Wales, found in the sandy soils of the coast and tablelands of the state.

RIGHT: Explorer Thomas Mitchell referred to Sulphur-crested Cockatoos as 'spirits of light'. They fly long distances if necessary to return to their roosts.

BELOW LEFT: The alpine flowers *Senecio lautus* are found in the mountainous areas of Australia, and flower throughout the year.

BELOW MIDDLE: Bright, colourful and highly visible, Rainbow Lorikeets gather in noisy flocks to feed, and are often frequent visitors to balconies and gardens in urban areas.

BELOW RIGHT: Golden Wattle is the floral emblem of Australia and one of 950 species of Acacia. Its yellow flowers are distinctive and fragrant.

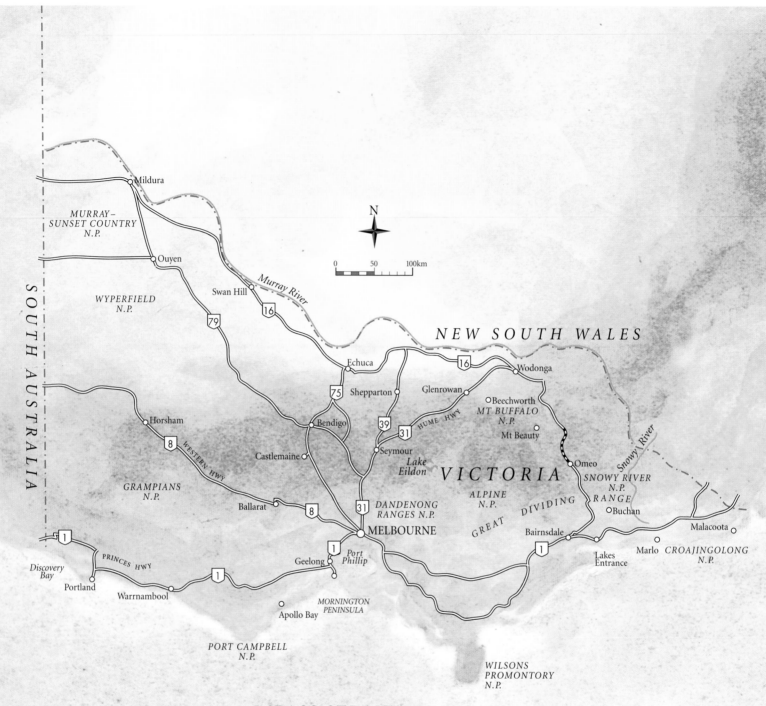

N

0   50   100km

MURRAY–
SUNSET COUNTRY
N.P.

Mildura

Ouyen

WYPERFIELD
N.P.

Swan Hill

79

16

Murray River

NEW SOUTH WALES

Echuca

16

Wodonga

75

Shepparton

Glenrowan

Beechworth

MT BUFFALO
N.P.

Horsham

39

31

HUME HWY

Mt Beauty

8

WESTERN HWY

Bendigo

Castlemaine

Seymour

Lake
Eildon

VICTORIA

Omeo

SNOWY RIVER
N.P.
RANGE

Snowy River

GRAMPIANS
N.P.

Ballarat

8

31

DANDENONG
RANGES N.P.

ALPINE
N.P.

GREAT   DIVIDING

Buchan

1

Warrnambool

Portland

Discovery
Bay

1

PRINCES HWY

MELBOURNE

1

Geelong

Port
Phillip

Bairnsdale

Lakes
Entrance

Marlo

Malacoota

CROAJINGOLONG
N.P.

SOUTH AUSTRALIA

Apollo Bay

MORNINGTON
PENINSULA

PORT CAMPBELL
N.P.

WILSONS
PROMONTORY
N.P.

BASS STRAIT

SOUTHERN
OCEAN

Victoria

Victoria is remarkable not only for its diverse landscapes, but also its historic past, a legacy of the boom days of the gold rushes. Today's ethnically diverse population enjoys a lifestyle built around fashion, art, music, sport and entertainment.

The smallest of the mainland states and the most densely populated, it is home to almost five million people, most of whom live in the cosmopolitan capital, Melbourne. With its Victorian heritage and a commitment to progress, the city is a combination of elegance and commercial pizzazz. Bestowed with natural attractions and elegant parks, the city sits astride the Yarra River, with sheltered beaches in the south and the west and the bush-clad slopes of the Dandenong Ranges to the east.

Straddling the river and bordered to the west by Port Phillip Bay, the city and adjacent Mornington Peninsula are close to seaside activities—swimming, windsurfing, sailing and fishing.

Victoria was first settled in 1833 at Portland on the south-west coast, by Edward Henty. By 1851 the population was confident enough to break away from the rule of New South Wales and soon prospered from the gold rush around Ballarat and Bendigo in the 1850s. The Eureka Uprising, a battle between the military and the gold diggers in 1854, is regarded by Victorians as the beginning of democracy in the fledgling colony. Victoria still has a strong economy, founded on business, financial, research and rural enterprises.

In the south of the state are the nature reserves of Phillip Island at the entrance to Western Port Bay, home of a Koala Conservation Centre and more than 250 species of birds including Pelicans, Ibis and Swans. A protected colony of Fairy Penguins parades to their burrows each evening. On the mainland, spectacular granite formations on Wilson's Promontory contrast with the sweep of Ninety Mile Beach and the azure waters of the Gippsland Lakes to the east where there are native forests, mountain ranges, beaches and waterways.

The Great Ocean Road, one of the world's great scenic drives along rugged coastal cliffs, was built in the 1920s by ex-servicemen using hand picks, shovels and horses and carts. It stretches from Torquay near Geelong to Apollo Bay, where the road winds

ABOVE: At sunrise, picturesque Lake Boga, near Swan Hill, is a tranquil oasis. By day, however, the water is a hive of activity, with swimming, sail-boarding, fishing and jet-skiing entertaining holidaymakers. During World War II, the lake was equally busy as the location of the flying boat repair depot, which operated between 1942 and 1947.

through lush rainforest, then reveals the impressive sea-ravaged limestone formations of Port Campbell National Park.

The alpine terrain to the north-east, on the border of New South Wales, is known as Snowy River Country, popular with skiers in the winter, and in summer a haven for bush walkers and fishermen. This is the source of the 2 600 kilometre Murray River that forms the border of Victoria and New South Wales until it meets the Southern Ocean near Goolwa in South Australia. Paddlesteamers ply the river and heritage ports line its banks, reminiscent of bygone days.

One of Australia's most infamous outlaws, Ned Kelly, is immortalised in bushranger country near the New South Wales border. The Kelly Gang controlled the town of Glenrowan in the 1880s, forcing a seige until the gang was dead and Kelly was tried and hanged. His exploits are legendary among every Australian schoolchild.

The comparatively small size of Victoria means that none of the state's modern and vibrant cities are too inaccessible. Nevertheless, there is still a sense of the state's wild past, of bushrangers and gold prospectors, and the pioneering spirit which nurtured the present-day prosperity.

LEFT: Sophisticated and cultured, Melbourne is Australia's second largest city and the grand old lady of the nation. Founded in 1835, the city prospered from the gold rushes of the 1850s and soon became the financial and social capital of the country. Much of the impressive Victorian architecture dating from these boom days still nestles among the buildings of the modern city.

ABOVE: Encircled by the giant towers of the secular world, St Patrick's Cathedral soars heavenwards, a spiritual icon of the city. An outstanding example of Gothic Revival architecture, St Patrick's is the largest cathedral in Australia.

BELOW LEFT: Melbourne trams have become symbols of the city. First put into operation in 1885, they have been a vital form of transport for visitors and Melburnians ever since.

BELOW RIGHT: The sounds, sights and smells of Chinatown, in Little Bourke Street, are an integral part of Melbourne's character. It is an area that reflects the importance of the ethnic community in Melbourne's history, having been continuously inhabited by the Chinese since the gold rushes of the 1850s.

ABOVE: With its great flight of steps leading to a colonnade of Doric pillars, Parliament House is the epitome of 19th century civic architecture. Built in 1856, but never completed, the interior is as lavish as the exterior is grand. The building houses the Legislative Council and Legislative Assembly.

LEFT: On the banks of the Yarra River, Melbourne's Crown Casino is a tubular, steely-grey building which opened in 1997. The building is virtually a city under one roof, offering food, shops, entertainment and—of course—gambling.

ABOVE: Exquisite parks and gardens are an integral part of Melbourne, and among these is Fitzroy Gardens, north of the city centre. Featuring flower displays, statues, a model Tudor village and even a fairy tree, the gardens are popular with Melburnians and a particular favourite with children.

TOP RIGHT: Melbourne's Royal Botanic Gardens are a magnificent spectacle and an oasis of tranquility amid the hustle and bustle of the city. Founded over 150 years ago, the gardens are renowned for their elegant lakes and rolling lawns, such as the Oak Lawn where many of the majestic trees are over a century old.

RIGHT: Cook's Cottage, in Fitzroy Gardens, dates from 1755 and was built in Great Ayton, England, as the family home of Captain James Cook's parents. In 1933, the building was dismantled and given to the state of Victoria as a centenary gift and a tribute to an outstanding navigator.

TOP: Ornate and expansive, the Windsor Hotel is a remnant of a bygone era, when society indulged its love of luxury in lavishly decorated public buildings. Built between 1883 and 1884, the Windsor is one of the few grand old hotels still remaining in Australia.

ABOVE LEFT: Built in 1887, the Princess Theatre is one of Melbourne's most historic old buildings, with allegorical figures on the façade as one of its many interesting architectural details.

ABOVE RIGHT: An elegant feature of the south entrance of Melbourne's Exhibition Building is the Hochgurtel Fountain, built in Cologne by Joseph Hochgurtel. It is an allegorical representation of trade between nations, and the concepts of Commerce, Industry, Science and Art.

ABOVE: Soaring skyward, Melbourne's cityscape is an eclectic mix of modern glass and steel towers, and old stone and brick residences. Towering above the meandering Yarra River, the 20th century edifices that have grown up around the Victorian foundations dwarf the spires of St Paul's Cathedral and the dome of Flinders Street Station.

LEFT: Deep in the heart of Carlton, one of the city's oldest and most interesting suburbs, lies Faraday Street, which, like Lygon Street, is home to cafés, Italian restaurants and bakeries. Waves of immigration in the 1950s and 1960s saw scores of Italians settle here, and their influence clearly remains.

BOTTOM LEFT: During the first week of March, the popular recreation area of Albert Park becomes the focus of the car racing world. The four-day Australian Formula One Grand Prix is held here on a track that circles the lake, with the sports hall transformed into the pit area.

THIS PAGE: On the first Tuesday of November every year since 1861, a three-minute horse race has brought the country to a standstill. The Melbourne Cup is an Australian institution, and for those lucky enough to be present at Flemington Racecourse, it is an occasion to dress to the nines. Resplendent in top hat and tails, gentlemen escort elegant ladies, who wear an infinite variety of hats trimmed with feathers and bows. As the horses thunder down the track, the nation holds its breath in anticipation of a win, cheering on the victorious horse.

ABOVE: Beneath the Eiffel Tower-like spire, reaching 115 metres above St Kilda Road, is the Victorian Arts Centre. The complex comprises a theatre with three auditoriums—including Australia's largest stage—a circular concert hall, and the National Gallery of Victoria.

RIGHT: With its air of restrained elegance, Como is one of the most beautiful and historically significant Australian homes. The house grew from a simple brick villa, begun in 1847, to a magnificent edifice, successfully mixing Italianate splendour with colonial simplicity.

ABOVE: Standing 60 metres high, the dome of Melbourne's Exhibition Building was visible for several kilometres when construction was completed in 1880, in time for the Melbourne International Exhibition. One third of Victoria's population packed into the building on the opening day to view 32 000 exhibits from 29 countries.

LEFT: Rippon Lea is one of Australia's great 19th century estates, and is a national treasure. The fine Victorian mansion is set amid 14 acres of parkland, encompassing a lake with islands, a rose garden, an apple orchard and a grand fernery.

TOP: For over 100 years, Melburnians have headed to suburban St Kilda to have fun on the beach, and to promenade along the foreshore. Lining the seafront is an eclectic mix of cosmopolitan cafés and weathered boarding houses, creating a relaxed atmosphere that contributes to the area's popularity.

ABOVE: Characterised by its row of colourful beach huts perching on the sand, the suburb of Brighton is another popular seaside area, with panoramic views of Port Phillip Bay. In the early days of the colony, the area was earmarked as a possible location for a port.

ABOVE: The vines around Dixons Creek in the Yarra Valley were first planted in 1838. One of the largest vineyards in the region is the family-run operation, De Bortoli Winery. Here, cool climate viticulture produces fine red and white table wines that are among the best in the country.

LEFT: Clothed in ash forests, the Dandenong Ranges are just an hour's drive from Melbourne. In the valleys, sparkling streams water delicate wildflowers and ferns, while many a peaceful road winding through the hills is flanked by towering Mountain Ash, the world's tallest hardwood.

ABOVE: Fine parks and landscaped gardens extend along the shores of Lake Wendouree in Ballarat, a man-made lake which hosted the rowing events for the 1956 Olympic Games.

BELOW LEFT: The heady days of the gold rushes may have passed, but visitors to Sovereign Hill Goldmining Township, a vast outdoor museum, can take a step back in time to Ballarat of the 1850s. Visitors can experience an authentic streetscape as well as panning for gold on the diggings.

BELOW RIGHT: Bendigo, like Ballarat, was once a thriving gold town, and home to the famous mines of Central Deborah and Ironbark. Rosalind Park, with its fernery, lawns and statues, is a pleasant retreat, and a good vantage point from which to view the Victorian cityscape, which is possibly the best-preserved example of its kind in Australia.

THIS PAGE: With its wild coastline bordered by the famous Great Ocean Road, Port Campbell National Park contains some of the most breathtaking scenery in the country. Among several extraordinary rock formations is the Arch (above) and the row of large rocks known as the Twelve Apostles (top left), which rise majestically from the chill waters of the Southern Ocean. Erosion has caused many changes over the years to these rugged cliffs. Another rock formation known as London Bridge collapsed in 1990 into the choppy waters, leaving only an isolated piece of rock divided from the cliffs (left).

THIS PAGE: The southern extremity of the Great Dividing Range is better known as the Grampians —an area of wild beauty. Covering some 1000 square kilometres, the towering peaks are popular with rock climbers, while in the plunging valleys exquisite rainforests are kept verdant by the rushing water from sparkling waterfalls. In spring, over 200 varieties of native wildflowers burst into life, while during winter, snowfalls occasionally carpet the trees and hidden valleys.

ABOVE: A ride on a paddleboat along the Murray River conjures up romantic images of days gone by, when the river was a busy traffic route bringing prosperity to the towns that grew up on its banks. The steamers that churned their way up the river to Swan Hill and Echuca in 1853 were the first of the riverboat era, a golden age for Victoria that still lingers in spirit along the Murray.

ABOVE: At the centre of the area known as Sunraysia is the settlement of Mildura, on the banks of the Murray River. The well-irrigated fields and pastures around Mildura are fertile and lush, and as a result the district supplies 80 per cent of Australia's dried fruit, 15 per cent of its citrus fruit and 85 per cent of its winemaking grapes.

RIGHT: Besides bringing wealth to Victoria, the discovery of gold also brought trouble. Gangs of bushrangers roamed the countryside, robbing and murdering as they went. The most famous of these fugitives was Ned Kelly, who was finally captured in Glenrowan where a statue and characters in costume commemorate this legendary figure from Australian history.

THIS PAGE: East of the Albury–Wodonga area, the landscape around Tallangatta (above) and Tintaldra (left) becomes heavily undulating, with fertile plains watered by cool rivers supporting agricultural activities ranging from dairy farms to hop growing. Pine forests are also dotted throughout the region, providing the raw material for paper and timber mills.

ABOVE: Covering almost all of Australia's alpine environment, Victoria's Alpine National Park is the largest in the state and includes spectacular, snow-capped mountains such as Mount Feathertop. The snowfields are the main attraction here, but the area also boasts more than 1100 native plant species.

RIGHT: Falls Creek is the state's second largest ski resort, located on the edge of the Bogong High Plains, within the Alpine National Park. Spectacularly situated near some of the highest peaks, the resort grew from a single hut built by workers on the Kiewa Hydro-electric Scheme.

BELOW RIGHT: Mount Buller Alpine Resort, 250 kilometres north-east of Melbourne, embodies spectacular alpine scenery. In winter, 180 hectares of ski trails are serviced by 27 ski lifts.

TOP: In the heart of the Victorian Alps, Mount Hotham is the country's highest ski resort. It is also a place of wide, dramatic skies where nature is at its wildest and most expressive.

ABOVE: In the evening light of summer, the view across the Alps is breathtaking. Alpine Ash forests line the slopes of the mountains, and in spring the meadows abound with wildlflowers.

LEFT: The shack known as Craig's Hut, which sits atop Mount Stirling, looks authentic but was in fact a film set used in the classic Australian adventure *The Man from Snowy River*.

ABOVE: In the foothills of the Alps lies the historic former gold-mining town of Beechworth, characterised by its Victorian architecture. Several buildings, constructed from the local honey-coloured granite, such as the old post office with its Italianate clock tower and belfry, have been classified by the National Trust.

RIGHT: The Beechworth cemetery contains many historic graves, including those of hundreds of Chinese who died during the Buckland Valley massacre of 1857. Among the graves are Chinese burning towers, used during funeral services to burn paper prayers, crackers and incense.

ABOVE: Mount Buffalo National Park is an area of exquisite beauty, with crystal streams, dainty wildflowers and ancient granite tors. Mount Buffalo itself, so named by Hume and Hovell in 1824 because of its resemblance to a buffalo, is an area of rocky outcrops weathered over millions of years.

LEFT: Located in the high country of the Upper Goulburn Valley, Lake Eildon is Victoria's largest man-made body of water, created in the 1950s to supply water to 8000 square kilometres of farmland. It is a picturesque sight in all weathers, particularly at dawn and dusk when kangaroos come to drink at the lake's edge.

ABOVE: Malacoota Inlet is renowned for its quiet beaches and waterways, and its excellent fishing. First settled in 1841, and used by whalers and sealers during the 19th century, the fishing village at the mouth of the inlet is now a popular seaside resort.

BELOW: The area around the small timber town of Buchan, in the far east of the state, is famous for its spectacular limestone caves, and at Buchan South a black marble outcrop was excavated for use in the construction of the 16 huge pillars for Melbourne's Shrine of Rememberance.

ABOVE: The most easterly part of Victoria is a place of spectacular cliffs, forest-covered peaks and small centres of population, through which winds the Snowy River, the area's main waterway. Green pastures line the river.

RIGHT: The small town of Bairnsdale, on the Mitchell River, is a settlement in Gippsland and is home to a remarkable building—St Mary's Catholic church, with walls and ceiling covered in murals painted by an Italian, Frank Floriani, during the Depression.

ABOVE: Wilson's Promontory, known affectionately to locals as the Prom, is the most southerly exten-sion of mainland Australia, and an area of unspoiled natural beauty, featuring numerous ancient rock formations. Some of the state's best beaches are found here along 130 kilometres of rugged coastline. Inland are lush tree-fern gullies, open heath and marshes and giant Mountain Ash trees.

ABOVE: One of the most striking features of the Grampians National Park is its rich and varied display of colourful wildflowers.

LEFT: The Kookaburra, with its characteristic 'laugh', is a well-known Australian bird, which feeds mainly on large insects, mice, small birds and small snakes.

BELOW LEFT: Rarely spotted in the wild, the Platypus is a shy creature whose habitat is the rivers and lakes of Australia's east coast.

BELOW MIDDLE: Melbourne's Fitzroy Gardens feature many stunning flower displays which are particularly colourful during spring.

BELOW RIGHT: Kangaroos are widespread across Australia and usually occur in mobs of fifty or more. They can hop at speeds of over 40 kilometres-per-hour.

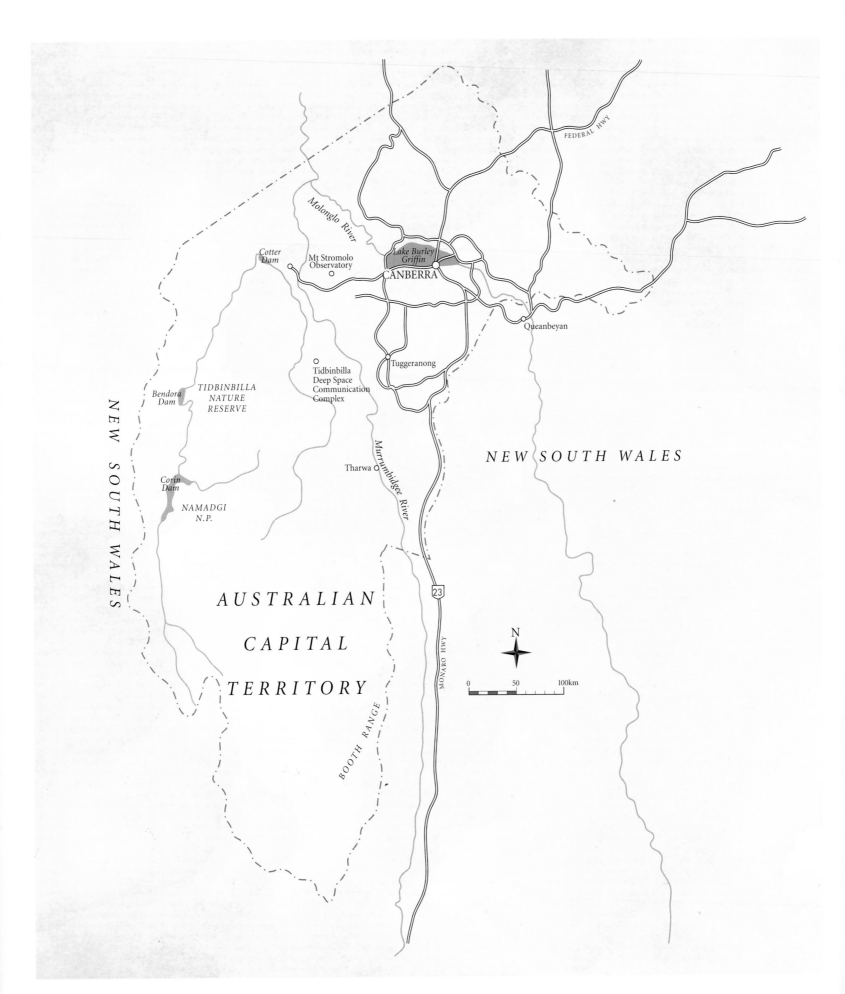

Molonglo River

Cotter
Dam

Mt Stromolo
Observatory

Lake Burley
Griffin

CANBERRA

Queanbeyan

Tuggeranong

TIDBINBILLA
NATURE
RESERVE

Bendora
Dam

Tidbinbilla
Deep Space
Communication
Complex

NEW SOUTH WALES

Corin
Dam

NAMADGI
N.P.

Tharwa

Murrumbidgee River

NEW SOUTH WALES

AUSTRALIAN

CAPITAL

TERRITORY

FEDERAL HWY

N

23

MONARO HWY

BOOTH RANGE

0   50   100km

Australian Capital Territory

Born of rivalry between Sydney and Melbourne, and sited between the two cities, Canberra has made history as a purpose-built national capital, setting its own style as a visionary urban community in a specially created state— the Australian Capital Territory.

The city's modern buildings, spacious tree-lined streets and picturesque lake are a tribute to Canberra's innovative designer, the American architect Walter Burley Griffin. Together with his wife Marion, Burley Griffin designed a geometrically-proportioned city around a lake, subsequently named in their honour, created by damming the Molonglo River. Landlocked within south-eastern New South Wales, the self-governing territory measures just 80 kilometres from north to south and about 30 kilometres wide.

Canberra is home to the head offices of government departments and most employment in the city is in the public service. Around 310 000 people enjoy the lifestyle of a well-planned urban development with modern facilities in an area surrounded by rolling hills and forests.

The centrepiece of the city is its famous fountain jet, the Captain Cook Memorial, in Lake Burley Griffin. On the southern side of the lake, the soaring flagmast of Parliament House dominates the skyline, the building blending with the summit of Capital Hill. The centre of government is encircled by spacious parks and administrative buildings including the National Gallery, National Library and High Court.

As the capital of the nation, Canberra showcases the best in exhibitions and entertainment. In addition, visitors can see elite athletes training at the Australian Institute of Sport, explore the cosmos at the Deep Space Communications Complex, watch the process of justice at the High Court of Australia or experience scientific phenomena at Questacon, the National Science and Technology Centre.

The city is endowed with 27 parks of bush and grassland, including the lakeside wetlands of Canberra Nature Park, and the Australian National Botanic Gardens with a collection of over 6 000 native plants. Further around the lake's northern shoreline is Commonwealth Park, venue for the renowned spring festival,

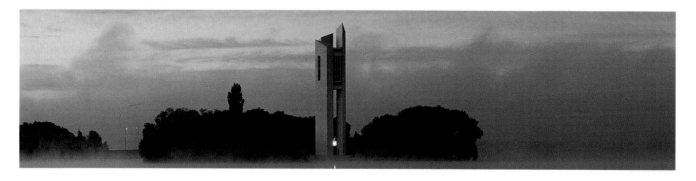

ABOVE: The jewel-pink hues of first light soften the stark lines of the Carillon on Lake Burley Griffin. A gift from the British Government in 1963 to mark Canberra's 50th anniversary, the three-column tower has 53 chimes that peal every 15 minutes.

Floriade, when the park is a blaze of colour with thousands of spring blooms transforming the grounds into a magical landscape.

Between Mount Ainslie in the Canberra Nature Park and the northern shore of Lake Burley Griffin is the Australian War Memorial, a tribute to the country's war dead, and the focus of the nation's annual Anzac Day commemoration on 25 April. The centrepiece of the Byzantine sandstone shrine, opened in 1941, is the domed Hall of Memory, surrounded by an art gallery, library and museum housing more than three million items.

The suburbs and farming communities within the Australian Capital Territory blend seamlessly with country New South Wales, where scenic rural villages and historic towns recall the region's past. The Gudgenby Nature Reserve to the south preserves native bush and wildlife and the landscape reflects the hues of the changing seasons, particularly evident in summer when the highland slopes are bright with wild-flowers. The region is traversed by the Molonglo and Murrumbidgee rivers and to the west is the Brindabella Range, extending to the slopes of the Snowy Mountains.

In the endless landscape of the southern tablelands there are magnificent homesteads and humble cottages; vast holdings for sheep, goats, cattle and alpacas; vineyards and wineries around Murrumbateman; potato farms at Crookwell; and wheatfields around the twin towns of Harden–Murrumburrah.

Combining past and future in a planned and progressive region, Canberra and the Australian Capital Territory reflect the dynamism of Australia in the 21st century.

LEFT: Parliament House, Australia's centre of government, glows in Canberra's evening light. Kings Avenue leads from the city across Lake Burley Griffin to the sweeping lawns in front of the forecourt and the illuminated flagpole shines out against the silhouetted hills.

TOP: The impressive entrance to Parliament House, illuminated by Australia's colours of green and gold, takes on a surreal glow under a full moon in the night sky.

ABOVE: Spectacular multi-coloured hot air balloons drifting silently over Lake Burley Griffin are captured between the sweeping lines of the Commonwealth Avenue Bridge.

RIGHT: The Canberra Deep Space Communication Complex at Tidbinbilla is a NASA facility, which receives and sends information between space-craft and research scientists.

ABOVE: Past, present and future create a time line in this vista of the Parliamentary Triangle. Across the lake is the elegant Old Parliament House, now the National Portrait Gallery, with the impressive lines of the new Parliament House appearing to embrace the vista as it rises behind it. To the left is the National Gallery and on the right is Questacon, the National Science and Technology Centre.

BELOW: Walter Burley Griffin, the American architect who designed Canberra, is commemorated in the name of Canberra's large, man-made body of water—Lake Burley Griffin. The lake was formed in 1964 when the Molonglo River was dammed, and today is a popular recreation area for water sports, cycling and walking.

RIGHT: At the top of Anzac Parade is the Australian War Memorial, officially opened on 11 November 1941. The building features exhibitions on wars in which Australia has participated, the tomb of the unknown soldier and a roll of honour lists the names of all Australians who have given their lives for their country.

BELOW: Among the places of interest around Lake Burley Griffin is the fountain known as the Captian Cook Memorial Water Jet. It springs from the centre of Lake Burley Griffin and reaches over 100 metres in height. Nearby, at Regatta Point, Cook's voyages are traced on a large globe.

LEFT: The landmark 195-metre Telstra Tower can be seen across Canberra on the summit of Black Mountain, near the Australian National Botanic Gardens to the north of Lake Burley Griffin. The tower is a communications link for the whole country.

BELOW: Appearing to float on the shimmering waters of Lake Burley Griffin, the glass and concrete edifice of the High Court of Australia houses three courtrooms and administrative offices. The highest court in the land, it is renowned for its impressive architecture, with a 24-metre high Great Hall at the centre of the building.

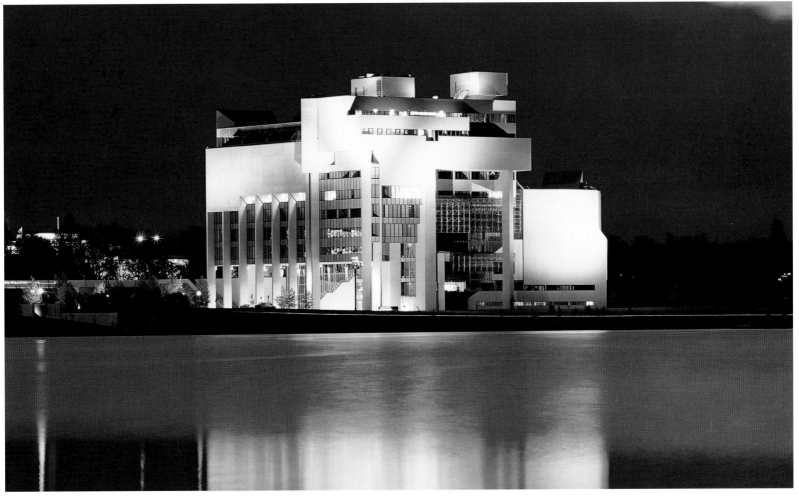

RIGHT: Against the cloudless sky an airship is dwarfed by a statue of an eagle with wings spread, on the pinnacle of the Australian–American Memorial in Thomas Blamey Square. At the centre of the Defence Department complex at Russell, it commemorates the contribution made by the people of the United States to the defence of Australia in World War II.

BELOW: Behind high white walls in Adelaide Avenue, Deakin, is The Lodge, a gracious homestead set in picturesque gardens that has been the official residence of successive Prime Ministers since 1927.

ABOVE: Magnificent marble columns frame the five-storeyed National Library of Australia, with its collections of books, maps, films, newspapers and paintings. Opened in 1968, the library has more than seven million books. The Henry Moore sculpture in the foreground is one of many valuable art works in its collections.

LEFT: Perfectly balanced in bronze, this statue of a gymnast by John Robinson represents just one of the range of sports coached at the Australian Institute of Sport in Bruce. Australia's elite athletes train at the complex of stadia and outdoor facilities.

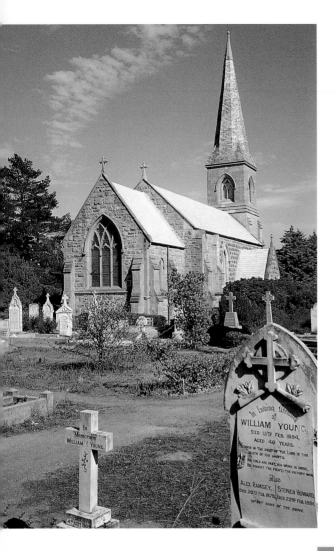

ABOVE LEFT: Governors–General have traditionally worshipped at the bluestone and sandstone church of St John the Baptist in Reid, built in the 1840s. The church has memorials to pioneering families and one of the earliest Australian-made stained glass windows. Old gravestones record the deaths of early residents.

ABOVE RIGHT: Blundell's Cottage was built in 1858 by a bullock driver who raised a family of eight in the house, on the Duntroon Estate. The restored stone building houses an exhibition on farming history.

RIGHT: Historic Duntroon House at the Royal Military Academy was built in 1862 and now houses the officers' mess. The Duntroon Military College, established in 1911, stands alongside the Australian Defence Force Academy, the tertiary training institution for all three armed services, established in 1986.

ABOVE: Native Bluebells appear in their thousands in the damp areas of the mountains in late summer and are the floral symbol of the Australian Capital Territory.

LEFT: Along with the Kangaroo, the Emu appears on Australia's coat-of-arms. It is a flightless bird but can run at speeds of up to 50 kilometres per hour.

BELOW LEFT: The colourful Eastern Rosella is found mainly in open woodlands, and is a ground-feeding seed-eater.

BELOW MIDDLE: Wild Coreopsis is often found in disturbed bushland in cooler areas of Australia. It flowers in spring.

BELOW RIGHT: The Galah, a distinctive pink and grey parrot, is one of the most abundant and familiar birds in Australia.

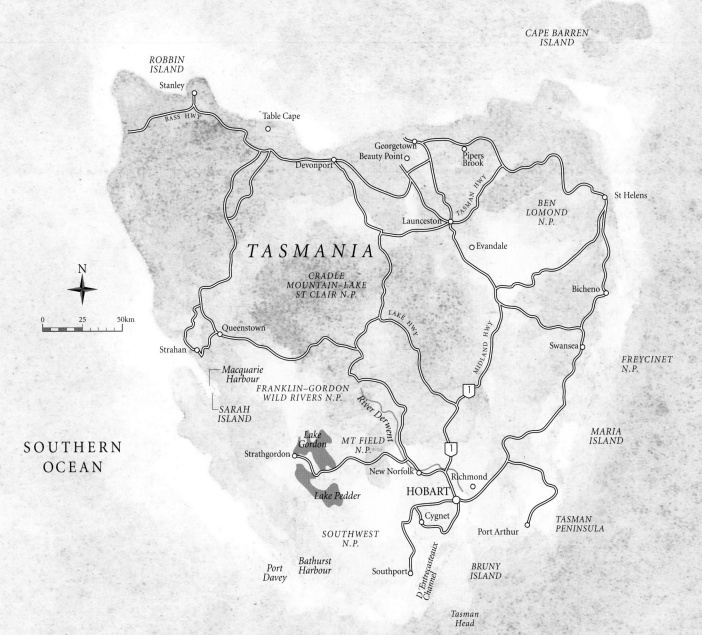

TASMAN
SEA

*FLINDERS
ISLAND*

Whitemark

Lady Barron

*CAPE BARREN
ISLAND*

BASS STRAIT

*ROBBIN
ISLAND*

Stanley

BASS HWY

Table Cape

Georgetown
Beauty Point

Pipers
Brook

Devonport

St Helens

TASMAN HWY

*BEN
LOMOND
N.P.*

Launceston

N

Evandale

TASMANIA

*CRADLE
MOUNTAIN–LAKE
ST CLAIR N.P.*

Bicheno

0   25   50km

LAKE HWY

Queenstown

MIDLAND HWY

*Macquarie
Harbour*

Strahan

Swansea

*FREYCINET
N.P.*

*FRANKLIN–GORDON
WILD RIVERS N.P.*

*SARAH
ISLAND*

*MARIA
ISLAND*

River Derwent

*Lake
Gordon*

*MT FIELD
N.P.*

SOUTHERN
OCEAN

Strathgordon

1

Richmond

New Norfolk

HOBART

Lake Pedder

1

Cygnet

Port Arthur

*TASMAN
PENINSULA*

*SOUTHWEST
N.P.*

D'Entrecasteaux Channel

*BRUNY
ISLAND*

*Port
Davey*

*Bathurst
Harbour*

Southport

*Tasman
Head*

84 PORTRAIT OF AUSTRALIA

Tasmania

Tasmania, Australia's smallest state, has a unique landscape, much of it unspoilt wilderness. The scars of its colonial past are still evident among the forested plains, where glassy blue glacial lakes mirror towering dolerite peaks. Separated from the mainland by the 240-kilometre wide Bass Strait, Tasmania is one of the most mountainous islands in the world with much of its windswept terrain lying at more than 1000 metres above sea level.

Once regarded as the most distant outreach of the British Empire, Hobart, at the mouth of the Derwent River, was founded by Lieutenant-Governor David Collins in 1804. As the second oldest capital city in Australia, it is an intriguing blend of old-world charm and modern day vitality, with the cloud-topped Mount Wellington looming in the background. The city claims a number of 'firsts'—it opened Australia's first legal casino at Wrest Point in 1973, while more than 100 years ago, the fledgling city also opened the country's first brewery, Cascade, in 1824, and Australia's first theatre, the Theatre Royal, in 1837.

Hobart is world-famous as the finishing line for the annual Sydney to Hobart Yacht Race, when the competing ocean yachts are at the mercy of the unpredictable seas and changeable weather in Bass Strait. The yachts sail into Constitution Dock, where dockside sandstone warehouses at Battery Point reflect the city's heritage. Georgian architecture in nearby Salamanca Place forms a backdrop to a Saturday outdoor market and workmen's cottages recall a way of life from the not-so-distant past.

Tasmania's original name, Van Dieman's Land, is synonymous with its status as a British penal outpost in the early 19th century. Convicts were detained in harsh conditions in such places as Macquarie Harbour; the so-called Female Factory, a women's prison in South Hobart; and solitary Sarah Island on the west coast. These places, where convicts outnumbered free settlers, became notorious for their brutal and oppressive regimes. At Port Arthur, the most famous and best preserved convict site, the ruins of the gaunt buildings on the green hills of the Tasman Peninsula are a reminder of its turbulent history.

Bruny Island, south of Hobart, was named after an early visit by the French explorer Bruni D'Entrecasteaux who chartered the waters in 1792. A picturesque haven for wildlife, the state's first

ABOVE: Tranquil Lake Pedder reflects the craggy slopes of the Frankland Ranges in the rugged wilderness of the Southwest National Park. The lake was flooded by the Hydro-Electric Commission in 1972, and is now many times its original size.

apple tree was planted here by Captain Bligh in 1791. The Huon Valley, across the channel, is renowned for apple and fruit orchards and the softwood Huon Pine. Further north is the mountainous peninsula of Freycinet National Park with its rare and distinctive formations of pink granite.

Beautiful beaches and fishing sites define the eastern coastline with historic echoes in its convict-built roads and bridges. Launceston, in the north of the state, sheltered in the upper reaches of the Tamar River, is Australia's third oldest city and was founded in 1805. An agricultural centre, it is the site of Australia's oldest woollen mill, opened in 1874. Near the centre is Cataract Gorge, a spectacular wilderness ravine.

The rugged west coast of Tasmania is remote and storm-battered, with soaring peaks shrouded in mist, and glacial lakes, a vestige of the island's origins in the last Ice Age. Minerals were mined here and national parks are home to Wallabies, Potoroos and Quolls, the Platypus and Echidna as well as the unique Tasmanian Devil, a carnivorous marsupial.

Much of Tasmania's impenetrable wilderness lies in the south-west, in the World Heritage-listed Cradle Mountain–Lake St Clair area. The icy waters of Lake St Clair form the deepest natural glacial lake in Tasmania and Mount Ossa is the highest mountain in the state. Much of the vast Southwest National Park remains unspoilt, with dense bush and mist-shrouded mountain ranges. The outstanding beauty of the Franklin–Gordon Wild Rivers National Park, in the midwest, is a testament to environmental groups who campaigned against the damming of Tasmania's great wild river, the Franklin.

Although proud of their important role in the making of modern Australia, Tasmanians take pride in their individuality and the distinctive character of their island state.

LEFT: Magnificently situated on the Derwent River, Hobart by night nestles in the glow of its twinkling lights against the backdrop of Mount Wellington. The second oldest city in Australia, it was founded by Colonel David Collins in 1804.

ABOVE: The plush Hotel Grand Chancellor overlooks both Constitution and Victoria docks. Here, in Victoria Dock, fishing boats lie at anchor around the harbour, while Constitution Dock plays host once a year to the Sydney–Hobart Yacht Race fleet.

RIGHT: In the midst of Franklin Square, a peaceful inner-city haven, is a memorial statue of Sir John Franklin, an early Governor of Tasmania. The small park was laid out in the 1860s.

ABOVE: Besides being a distinctive landmark of Hobart, the Tasman Bridge is the major arterial link between the city's eastern and western shores. In 1975 the bridge broke in two when a cargo ship crashed into one of its pylons.

LEFT: The elegant sandstone building of the Cascade Brewery is picturesquely situated in South Hobart, with the tree-clad slopes of Mount Wellington in the distance. In operation since 1824, Cascade is the oldest brewery in Australia.

ABOVE: At 340 metres above sea level, the lookout at Mount Nelson offers superb views of the Derwent River estuary as it winds around the city. In 1811, a signal station was established on this vantage point to announce the arrival of ships into Storm Bay. The building in the foreground is Wrest Point, Australia's first legal casino.

BELOW LEFT: The Georgian sandstone warehouses of Salamanca Place are regarded as Australia's finest examples of dockside architecture. Faithfully preserved, the buildings and their surrounding cobblestone streets now house cafés and art galleries, and a Saturday market.

BELOW RIGHT: Bridge Street in the historic township of Richmond is steeped in convict and colonial history. There are many old buildings along the cobblestone and slate streets, now mostly lined with tea rooms, galleries, craft and antiques shops.

ABOVE: Visitors to Richmond could be forgiven for thinking they were in the English countryside. This charming rural idyll is the site of the oldest bridge in Australia, convict built in 1823; and the oldest Catholic church, set among green pastures and rolling hills.

LEFT: Amid the hopfields that march in ranks across the Derwent Valley are these oast houses, used to dry the hops after harvesting. Steeped in character, they look is if they have been plucked straight out of the English countryside. The valley is the centre of the state's hopgrowing industry.

ABOVE: Port Cygnet, a five-kilometre inlet of the Huon River, leads to the small town of Cygnet, where shipyards opened early last century are still in business. As its name suggests, the town and its port were named by French explorer D'Entrecasteaux because of the number of swans he saw here.

TOP: Coles Bay, in Freycinct National Park, is overshadowed by the four peaked ridges known as the Hazards. The park covers 13 000 hectares of coastal heaths, dry open woodlands and forests.

ABOVE: Hastings, south of Hobart, is renowned for its three limestone caves, discovered in 1917. The most famous of these, the Newdegate Cave, with its delicate stalactite formations, has been described as one of the most beautiful in the country.

LEFT AND BOTTOM LEFT: The unusually named Bust-Me-Gall and Break-Me-Neck hills were so-called by John de Courcy Harte, reputedly an oft-drunken Irishman who was granted land in Swanport in 1821, and who must have experienced difficulty climbing these hills!

ABOVE LEFT: The now ruined Port Arthur church was once a part of the penal colony set amid the beautiful surroundings of the Tasman Peninsula. Prisoners attended services here until the colony closed in 1878, and in 1997 a memorial service was held among the ruins for the victims of the 1996 Port Arthur massacre.

ABOVE RIGHT: The ruins of the 1842 Port Arthur hospital are another dominant reminder of the penal colony. Convicts and soldiers were treated here, in separate wards, while free men and officers were afforded the luxury of being treated in their own homes.

BELOW: The picturesque Derwent River winds through a valley that is often likened to rural England. The beauty of the valley changes with the seasons, and along its banks orchards and fertile farmlands combine with the rustic towns and villages to create a vision of a rural paradise.

ABOVE: North of Binalong Bay on the east coast, near St Helens, is the intriguingly named Bay of Fires—so called from the early sightings of fires lit by local Aborigines. Now, the lichen-encrusted boulders give off a fiery hue of their own.

LEFT: The jagged, steep cliffs of the Ben Lomond Range, at 1300 metres high, dominate the horizon and loom over the surrounding Ben Lomond National Park. This is also the site of the state's main skiing area, operational during the months of July through to September.

ABOVE: Australia's third oldest city, Launceston, is located on the Tamar River below Mount Barrow. Founded in 1805, the city took its name from Launceston in Cornwall, the birthplace of Governor Phillip Gidley King.

BELOW LEFT: In keeping with the heritage of the surrounding area, visitors to Penny Royal World in Launceston can experience an Edwardian tram and underground working museum, as well as preserved 19th century mills, in a setting of picturesque lakes and waterfalls.

BELOW RIGHT: Located at the head of the Tamar River, only 64 kilometres from Bass Strait, Launceston is home to many boats and pleasure craft which are moored along the river. The South Esk River joins the Tamar at Launceston, providing a substantial network of waterways and making boating and cruising a popular pastime.

ABOVE: Hemmskirk Vineyard at Pipers Brook forms part of the largest concentration of vines in Tasmania. Chosen for its cool climate and similar conditions to the famous vine-growing areas of France, Pipers Brook wines are well-known among wine connoisseurs.

LEFT: Built in 1838, Clarendon, near the village of Nile, is a Tasmanian architectural showpiece. Its beautifully proportioned and harmonious design, a fine example of Regency architecture, is dominated by the two-storey portico supported by Ionic pillars. The interior is furnished in Georgian splendour.

ABOVE: At sunrise, as the yachts at anchor bob on the early morning tide and the gently rippling water catches the first rays of sun, it is not hard to see how Beauty Point got its name. A popular fishing and watersport centre, it was the original port for Beaconsfield, an 1879 gold town.

LEFT: Mount Roland, in the north of the state, dominates the surrounding farmland of the Kentish Plains, where softly undulating hills lead to the quiet streams and forests that are within easy reach.

ABOVE: Aromatic lavender carpets the foothills of the Sideling Ranges north-east of Launceston. The Bridstowe Estate Lavender Farm is the only source of true perfumery lavender outside Europe and is one of the largest in the world. The crop is harvested in early December to produce oil for the international perfume industry.

ABOVE: The small fishing port and historic town of Stanley, crouching below the rocky headland known as 'the Majestic Nut', is the oldest settlement in the north-west, dating back to 1826. Among the historic buildings that still remain is this 1830s bluestone Highfield chapel.

RIGHT: Among the high mountain ranges of the west coast, rich mineral deposits were discovered late last century. Mount Lyell, which is still operational, yields thousands of tonnes of copper, silver and gold.

BELOW: The landscape around Table Cape is lush and verdant, with farmland stretching right to the edge of the 115-metre cliffs. During spring, a bulb farm on top of Table Cape produces a colourful display of tulips in time for the annual tulip festival.

BELOW: Deep in the heart of the Southwest National Park is Port Davey, one of the remotest areas in Tasmania. Imposing fiord-like waterways extend into the park from Port Davey and Bathurst Harbour, which are regularly windswept by the gales and heavy rain of the Roaring Forties.

ABOVE: The Spotted-tail Quoll is a carnivorous marsupial, found almost exclusively in Tasmania.

LEFT: Tasmania is known as the Apple Isle for the quality and quantity of its apples.

BELOW LEFT: The Tasmanian Wombat is a large, burrowing nocturnal mammal, and is widespread throughout the state.

BELOW MIDDLE: Opium Poppies are commercially grown in Tasmania, producing a large percentage of world pharmaceutical requirements.

BELOW RIGHT: Cape Barren Geese are a rare species, living mostly on small, offshore islands.

OPPOSITE: Dove Lake, located in the Cradle Mountain–Lake St Clair National Park, is dominated by the serrated peak of Cradle Mountain.

NORTHERN TERRITORY

QUEENSLAND

WESTERN AUSTRALIA

GREAT VICTORIA DESERT

WITJIRA N.P.

SIMPSON DESERT

STURT STONY DESERT

Marla

87

Oodnadatta

Lake Eyre

LAKE EYRE N.P.

STRZELECKI DESERT

Coober Pedy

SOUTH AUSTRALIA

GAMMON RANGES N.P.

Lake Torrens

Lake Frome

NEW SOUTH WALES

NULLARBOR PLAIN

LAKE GAIRDNER N.P.

Lake Gairdner

Woomera

FLINDERS RANGES N.P.

Nullarbor

1

Ceduna

1

GREAT AUSTRALIAN BIGHT

Streaky Bay

Quorn

Port Augusta

32

Whyalla

Port Pirie

Cowell

EYRE PENINSULA

Burra

Murray River

Spencer Gulf

1

Renmark

Port Lincoln

YORKE PENINSULA

20

BAROSSA VALLEY

ADELAIDE

Murray Bridge

N

Gulf of St Vincent

12

FLINDERS CHASE N.P.

FLEURIEU PENINSULA

8

0   100   200km

KANGAROO ISLAND

Encounter Bay

Bordertown

VICTORIA

Robe

1

SOUTHERN OCEAN

Mt Gambier

South Australia

South Australia, the continent's driest state, is mostly comprised of the arid Outback desert country of the north, broken by rugged ranges and untamed bushy outcrops. By contrast, in the south, acres of vineyards produce top-quality wines, and the fertile lands watered by the Murray River yield abundant crops. In many parts of the state, a strong sense of heritage echoes the traditions of the early settlers.

The elegant capital, Adelaide, on the River Torrens, is Australia's fourth-largest city. A planned city of gracious design, it is a tribute to the fledgling colony's Surveyor-General, Colonel William Light. He selected the site for free settlers in 1836 and named it after Queen Adelaide, wife of King William IV. The spacious city centre, with its numerous heritage buildings, is surrounded by parkland and bordered by the hills of the Mt Lofty Ranges and the waters of the Gulf St Vincent.

Once named 'the City of Churches', today Adelaide is known as the Festival City. The biennial Adelaide Arts Festival attracts guest speakers and performers from all over the world while the concurrent Fringe Festival features alternative contemporary music and performance art. The biennial music festival, Womadelaide, is one of the premier world music events.

Not far from the capital is the fascinating Barossa Valley, a collection of towns, villages and wineries steeped in heritage and the traditions of lore. The first vineyard was planted in here 1847 by Lutherans who fled to Australia to escape Prussian persecution. They brought with them the rituals and customs of their homeland, which are still preserved by their descendants. The region is now home to more than 50 wineries, and is widely acknowledged to be one of the world's best wine-producing areas. Other important wine-growing regions are found in the south-east around Penola, Coonawarra and Padthaway; in the Clare Valley, north of the Barossa; and around McLaren Vale on the Fleurieu Peninsula.

Kangaroo Island, only 13 kilometres off shore, is Australia's third largest island, much of it empty wilderness and unsealed roads. One quarter of the island is covered by national parks, which are a haven for native wildlife—including an abundance of Kangaroos in Flinders Chase National Park.

ABOVE: After rain, the dry and barren landscape around Coober Pedy explodes with colour as myriad wildflowers bring the harsh outback terrain to life. All over the desert, hardy plants survive in the midst of an unforgiving land and an inhospitable climate.

The coast of South Australia, washed by the Southern Ocean, is broken by the three prongs of the Eyre, Yorke and Fleurieu peninsulas. The Mediterranean climate of the Fleurieu Peninsula makes it the state's fruit-growing area, with apple and pear orchards, vineyards and groves of olive and almond trees. The Yorke Peninsula is primarily an agricultural area, and the Eyre Peninsula a place of wild coastlines and small fishing towns and bays.

The world's longest walking path, the Heysen Trail, begins near the tip of the Fleurieu Peninsula at Cape Jervis and winds along coastal cliffs and national parks, ending 1500 kilometres to the north in the Parachina Gorge of the Flinders Ranges. In the midst of this unforgiving landscape is Wilpena Pound, a spectacular natural basin, ringed by 1000-metre cliffs and home to abundant wildlife and vegetation.

Australia is the world's richest opal-mining centre, and most of the mines are located in South Australia's Outback. The rugged town of Coober Pedy, on the Stuart Highway, is fringed by over 70 opal fields. The Aboriginal name given to the town means 'white fellow's hole in the ground', an apt description of this eccentric township, where many residents live in underground dugouts to shelter from the extreme temperatures.

To the west of the state are the red-ochre sands of the vast Nullarbor Plain, an empty stretch of land, and in fact the biggest block of limestone in the world, named from the Latin *nullus arbor*, meaning 'no trees'. The plateau merges seamlessly into the desolate desert country of Western Australia.

With a population of 1.5 million, South Australia is bordered by all of the mainland states. It is undoubtedly a place of contrasts, where the rawness of the Outback is little more than a naked country of vast horizons, but the south is gentle and cultured, steeped in history and as refined as the wines it produces.

LEFT: Adelaide is a gracious city, located on the picturesque banks of the River Torrens, surrounded by green parkland. Beyond the metropolitan district, the hills of the Mount Lofty Ranges shelter the city from the unrelenting Outback, stretching into the hinterland.

ABOVE: St Peter's Cathedral in North Adelaide, perfectly situated on sloping parkland, epitomises the elegance of the 'City of Churches'. Built in 1869 in French Gothic Revival style, it is characterised by its soaring twin spires, housing a set of eight bells reputed to be the heaviest in the southern hemisphere.

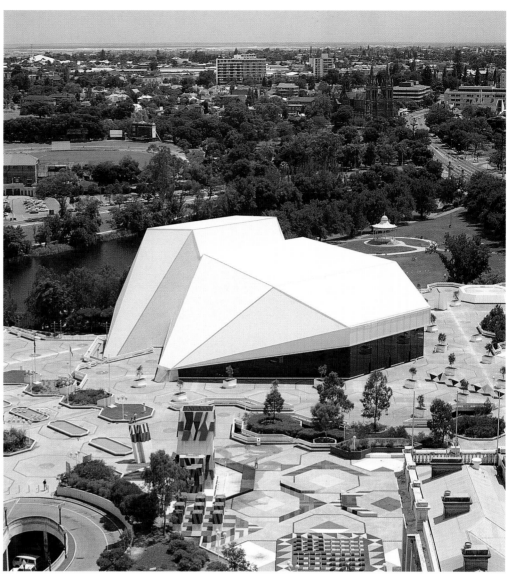

ABOVE: South Australia is known as the Festival State with good reason, and many of the state's larger cultural events are held beneath the white, angular roofs of the Festival Centre. The complex features several theatres and auditoriums, as well as an open-air amphitheatre.

LEFT: The city of Adelaide is laid out in a grid pattern, to the plan of the first Surveyor-General Colonel William Light. At its heart is Victoria Square—a pleasant interruption to the city's main thoroughfare, King William Street. The fountain is a favourite gathering place among locals, overlooked by the Hilton Hotel.

ABOVE: Australia's largest glasshouse, otherwise known as the Bicentennial Conservatory, houses a complete rainforest environment in a climate controlled by the conservatory's own cloud-making system. The surrounding Botanic Gardens are tranquil and spacious, with myriad exotic and native plants amid lawns and lakes.

BELOW LEFT: An easy stroll from the city centre is the suburb of North Adelaide, one of the older parts of the city, characterised by stately mansions and small, bluestone cottages. Interesting old pubs abound, such as the Lion Hotel on the corner of Melbourne and Jeringham streets.

BELOW RIGHT: Glenelg is Adelaide's suburban seaside resort. It is an enjoyable tram ride from the city, on board an original wood-panelled 1929 tram, to the site of the landing place of Governor Hindmarsh and the first South Australian colonists.

ABOVE: Flanking the city to the south and east, the Adelaide Hills district provides an escape to woods and parklands, where quiet vineyards sprawl across rolling hills and valleys. Small communities, such as Piccadilly, have a timeless, mellow quality, popular with locals and visitors alike.

LEFT: The McLaren Vale is one of the great wine regions of South Australia, and home to about 40 wineries, from which the grapes harvested year after year comprise a large percentage of the state's total output. Throughout the year, several festivals celebrate the viticultural delights of the area.

ABOVE AND RIGHT: Deep in the heart of the picturesque Clare Valley is the Bungaree merino stud, established in 1841. In addition to the elegant, two-storey homestead dating from 1869, is the historic woolshed, in which the farm's merino sheep are shorn.

ABOVE: At the tip of the Yorke Peninsula lies Innes National Park, a contrasting area of rough cliffs, wild beaches and sand dunes, and an interior of mallee scrub, salt lakes and marshes. A lighthouse sits atop Cape Spencer, near the old mining town of Inneston.

LEFT: Port Pirie is a busy, industrial port city and the fourth largest urban centre in South Australia. A surprising find amid the smelters' chimneys and wheat silos is the historic train station in the main street, built in the fashion of a Regency pavilion complete with ornate clock tower.

BOTTOM LEFT: The mine at Burra, dating from 1847, once produced five per cent of the world's copper. After the mine shut in 1877, Burra was transformed from a boisterous mining town to a quiet farming community, where the solid stone buildings impart an air of enduring charm which still lingers to this day.

RIGHT: The Eyre Peninsula is famous for its spectacular scenery, including the stretch of coastline known as the Whalers Way—a dramatic clifftop route that hugs the rugged shoreline from Fishery Bay to Cape Carnot. The name derives from a small whaling operation that existed here from 1837 to 1841.

BELOW LEFT: Port Lincoln began life in 1834 as one of the earliest settlements in South Australia, and today is a busy port—its harbour dotted with yachts and trawlers. The state's largest tuna fleet is based here, and fishing is a popular pastime as well as a thriving local industry.

BELOW RIGHT: To see a Southern Right Whale, frolicking in the waters of the Great Australian Bight, is to witness one of nature's finest moments. No longer hunted for their blubber oil and baleen, these mighty, magnificent mammals of the deep can safely pass on their long journey of migration north.

ABOVE: Southern Right Whales are often seen in Encounter Bay, near the town of Victor Harbor on the Fleurieu Peninsula. Here, once the site of three whaling stations, they were hunted to near-extinction during the peak whaling period. Now they have started to return, to the delight of scores of whale-watchers and conservationists.

LEFT: Flinders Chase National Park, on Kangaroo Island, is not only home to a plethora of native wildlife, but also to the aptly named Remarkable Rocks. Standing on a massive granite dome, these wind-sculpted shapes are the result of the erosive powers of wind, sea and rain over thousands of years.

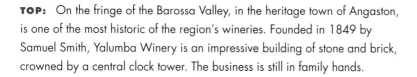

TOP: On the fringe of the Barossa Valley, in the heritage town of Angaston, is one of the most historic of the region's wineries. Founded in 1849 by Samuel Smith, Yalumba Winery is an impressive building of stone and brick, crowned by a central clock tower. The business is still in family hands.

ABOVE: Settled in 1839, Lyndoch is the southern gateway to the Barossa Valley and one of the oldest towns in the state. There are several wineries in and around Lyndoch, including Chateau Yaldara, which was transformed from the ruins of a flour mill into a splendid Baroque-style chateau.

RIGHT: The pretty town of Bethany, the Barossa's oldest settlement, was founded in 1842 by 28 Lutheran families who emigrated from Prussia. The old buildings and stone cottages remain, as does the Herberge Christi Church, where the bell is still rung at sunset to mark the end of the day's work.

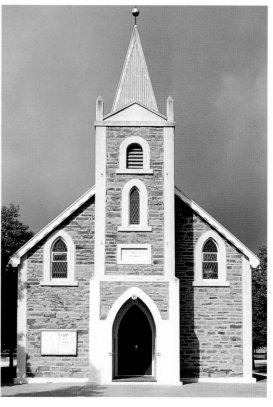

ABOVE: The world-renowned wines of the Barossa Valley are inextricably linked with its landscape. Picturesque and atmospheric, the valley is carpeted with hectares of meticulously maintained vineyards, dotted with thatched barns and church spires. It is a timeless land, shaped by the early settlers and their descendants, who planted the customs and traditions of their homeland along with the vines.

ABOVE: Wild and unspoilt, the ancient peaks of the Flinders Ranges form a craggy rampart around an area of incredible natural beauty. The semi-arid climate nurtures dry-country vegetation, such as salt-bush and light timber, while along the valley floor River Red Gums, White Cypress and Pepper-mint Box trees are common. The Flinders Ranges National Park comprises 78 000 hectares.

BELOW: Established in 1890, the sheep station at Cordillo Downs, in the far north-east corner of the state, is the stuff of which Australian legends are made. In its heyday, the station's 80 000 sheep produced 1000 bales of wool each year. Essential to this process was the shearing shed, built in an unusual barrel shape, with self-supporting short sheets of corrugated iron, due to the difficulty of transporting large sheets of iron across the desert, and the lack of timber.

LEFT: From high above Wilpena Pound, the view of the Flinders Ranges is an awe-inspiring spectacle of one of nature's most majestic creations. Winding southward, the serrated ridge of the ABC Range snakes across the landscape, like the tail of an enormous dragon, for as far as the eye can see. Far below, peaks and ridges are cut by valleys and twisting gorges, and cool creeks pass red-walled escarpments.

BELOW: In its heyday the small town of Quorn was a bustling place, a community that grew around a rail junction where lines from Perth, Broken Hill, Alice Springs and Adelaide converged. The line was eventually rerouted and today the Pichi Richi steam railway, run by enthusiasts, is the only train to chug along the small remaining section of the Old Ghan track.

TOP AND ABOVE: Coober Pedy is the centre of the world's opal industry, and one of the hottest places on earth. With temperatures often exceeding 50°C, much of the population live, work and worship underground to escape the fierce heat. The Serbian Orthodox Church is one of two underground churches in the town, complete with icons.

RIGHT: Above ground, the landscape around Coober Pedy is littered with abandoned mines and huge piles of mullock. Past these diggings, the highly coloured plateau known as the Breakaways is a continuation of this rather surreal terrain. Erosion has exposed large mounds of sand and rock spreading over an area of some 40 square kilometres.

ABOVE: The Murray River is Australia's Mississippi. From its origin in the Snowy Mountains, the river winds through green dairy flats and semi-arid plains on its 2588-kilometre journey to the Southern Ocean. A popular way to experience this mighty waterway is by a paddlesteamer such as the *Murray Princess*, which takes passengers on pleasure cruises between the Murray towns.

LEFT: South of Murray Bridge, the land along the banks of the Murray River is lush and well-irrigated, supporting dairy cattle and bountiful citrus crops. To the north, however, towns such as Walker Flat, perched on cliffs overlooking the river, are built on poorer soil (left), where the main crop is cereal grains.

BOTTOM LEFT: The Bleasdale Winery at Langhorne Creek, near Murray Bridge, is one of Australia's most historic wineries, with buildings classified by the National Trust and a wine press dating back to 1860. The winery is still in the hands of the Potts family, descendents of the founder Frank Potts, who arrived on HMS *Buffalo* as a midshipman in 1836 and founded the operation in 1850.

ABOVE: The Nora Creina scenic drive, in the south-east of the state, passes pristine coastline, small beaches, sand dunes and substantial saltwater and freshwater lakes. Rocky enclaves make picturesque fishing spots and the area is noted for its diversity of wildlife.

RIGHT: The Naracoorte caves, discovered in 1908, contain some of the most beautiful limestone formations in the country, including stalactites, stalagmites, helictites, straws, columns and flourstone. The mirror pool in the Alexandra Cave reflects the rocky sculptures, illuminated by coloured lights.

ABOVE LEFT: Australian Sea Lions spend as much time on land as at sea, and breed in summer. Approximately 6000 live and breed around Cape du Couedic.

ABOVE RIGHT: The flowers of the Yellow Gum tree can be cream, white or pink, and bloom in autumn. The tree is found in Victoria and South Australia.

BELOW LEFT: Found only in Australia and New Zealand, Fairy Penguins are the smallest species of penguin, and inhabit the wildlife haven of Kangaroo Island.

BELOW MIDDLE: Sturt's Desert Pea is the floral emblem of South Australia, found in arid inland areas.

BELOW RIGHT: The insect-eating Central Bearded Dragon defends itself by opening its mouth and pushing forward its throat skin to form a 'beard'.

TIMOR
SEA

INDIAN
OCEAN

N

0   100   200km

Wyndham
Kununurra
Lake
Argyle
KIMBERLEY
REGION
Derby
Broome
Fitzroy
Crossing
Halls Creek
PURNULULU
(BUNGLE
BUNGLE)
N.P.

GREAT SANDY
DESERT

Port Hedland

Karratha
Marble Bar

Exmouth

NORTH WEST COASTAL HWY

HAMERSLEY RANGE

LITTLE SANDY
DESERT

GIBSON DESERT

NORTHERN TERRITORY

WESTERN
AUSTRALIA

KARIJINI
N.P.
Newman

GREAT NORTHERN HWY

KENNEDY RANGE

Carnarvon

Monkey Mia

Zuytdorp
KALBARRI
N.P.
Kalbarri

Meekathana

95

GREAT VICTORIA
DESERT

Mt Magnet

Geraldton

95

Leonora

NULLARBOR PLAIN

SOUTH AUSTRALIA

1

Kalgoorlie–Boulder

Northam
94
PERTH
Fremantle
York

Norseman

EYRE HIGHWAY
Eucla

1

Bunbury
Margaret River
LEEUWIN–NATURALISTE
N.P.
STIRLING
RANGE
N.P.
1
Esperance

SOUTHERN
OCEAN

SOUTHERN
OCEAN

FITZGERALD
RIVER N.P.

D`ENTRCASTEAUX
N.P.
Albany

Western Australia

estern Australia, the continent's largest state, is a sea of vast landscapes dissolving into a distant shimmer of heat and light; endless blue skies and lonely distances; white foamed shores and sandy beaches; and rugged coastal cliffs swept by raging seas.

The state was first discovered by Dutch navigator Dirk Hartog in October 1616, but it was more than 200 years before Captain Charles Fremantle took possession of the Swan River territory for Britain on 2 May 1829. Settlers arrived on the transport ship *Parmelia*, and Captain James Stirling declared Fremantle as the settlement's port, founding Perth on 12 August 1829.

Riverside Perth, home to 1.38 million people, is the most isolated capital city in the world, as well as the fastest growing capital in the country. Among the modern buildings, the heritage of the early settlers is still evident in buildings such as the Fremantle Prison, Government House, the Perth Town Hall, the Meadow Street precinct at Guildford and the road between Perth and Albany. From 1850 the British Government sent convicts to construct roads and buildings, due to early difficulties in communication, problems with finance and a shortage of labour.

With its Mediterranean climate, long hours of sunshine, verdant parks and white sandy beaches lurking under an azure sky, Perth is an altogether pleasant place to live. The Swan River that meanders through Perth from its origins at the Port of Fremantle was named after the distinctive black birds discovered there more than 166 years ago. The riverside 400-hectare Kings Park is home to 250 species of plants, and during the months of September and October, wildflowers burst into bloom in a carpet of vibrant colour. There are more than 8000 species throughout the state.

With the longest coastline of the Australian states, stretching from the Timor Sea in the north, and the Indian Ocean in the west to the Great Southern Ocean, watersports are a way of life for West Australians. At Monkey Mia, near the westernmost point on the coast, even the Dolphins swim into shore. Whale watching is a favourite pastime on the Sunset Coast from August to November, when Humpback Whales and their young journey to Antarctica from the far north.

ABOVE: The pristine waters of Lake Argyle in the east Kimberley sustain diverse fauna and flora. The largest artificial lake in Australia, it was formed in 1972 as part of the Ord River Scheme to irrigate the unproductive countryside, which is now highly fertile.

Gold is the key to the heartlands of Western Australia—the gold of the wheatfields and rich agricultural land, and the gold of the mines in the Kalgoorlie–Boulder area. The first discovery of gold in Western Australia was at Halls Creek in the remote Kimberley in 1885, an area that has riches off the coast in pearls, and underground in gold, diamonds and minerals. Major strikes at Coolgardie and nearby Kalgoorlie saw a goldrush that established wealth and independence for the state.

In the north of the state are the surreal landscapes of the 350-million-year-old Bungle Bungle Range, and the awe-inspiring Kimberley, a wilderness still regarded as Australia's last frontier. In the south-west are found natural Jarrah and the famously-tall Karri trees, unique to Western Australia. Karri is a valuable timber, prized for its resistence to termites.

Spanning one-third of the Australian continent and encompassing a spectrum of climatic zones, Western Australia stretches over 2.5 million square kilometres, an area almost the same size as India. It is a place of rich, sunburnt colours, where arid desert lands yield unimaginable wealth—gold, iron ore, diamonds, gas and minerals. Much of the land beyond the coastal plain is endless and uninhabited, but West Australians revel in their isolation and their sense of independence from the more populous, eastern states.

LEFT: By night, the city of Perth sparkles like a jewel on dark velvet, as parklands and river form a background to the ribbon-lights of the Mitchell Freeway and the towering skyline of the central business district.

ABOVE: Black swans and cygnets drift on the reflective waters of one of the city's lakes, beneath the azure skies of a Perth afternoon. Spacious parkland surrounds the shopping and business precinct of high rise buildings.

RIGHT: Governor Stirling laid the foundation stone for the original flour mill for early settlers on the Swan River in 1835, but its working life was short-lived. It closed in 1859 when newer mills were built near the wheat-growing areas. The Narrows Bridge approach-roads wind around the mill and the restored building houses many old relics.

ABOVE LEFT: His Majesty's Theatre is an elegant Edwardian building, opened in 1904 and restored in 1979. Perth's first steel and concrete building, its highly decorated façade is a reminder of the architectural styles around the turn-of-the-century and contrasts with the soaring concrete and glass structures in the city.

ABOVE RIGHT: Cool waters reflect the cloisters of Winthrop Hall at the University of Western Australia, established in the 1930s in park-like grounds on the banks of the Swan River. Limestone blocks for the neo-classical buildings were quarried on site and the quarry itself transformed into an amphitheatre.

LEFT: Black swans lived on the river long before the area was discovered by white settlers and they remain an inspirational symbol of the city of Perth. Their importance is immortalised in the illuminated Swan Fountain (near the Burswood Casino) its colours captured in the full moon.

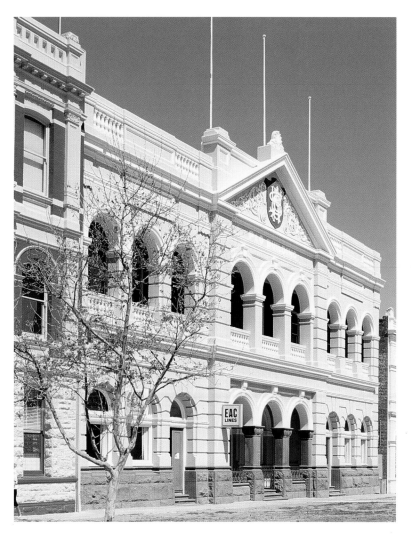

ABOVE LEFT: The historic port of Fremantle, settled before Perth, is a treasure trove of maritime history. These Victorian sandstone buildings were built for shipping lines and they are still used by the travel industry.

ABOVE RIGHT: Strawberry Hill, possibly Western Australia's oldest stone house, was built in 1836 for Sir Richard Spencer, the government representative at Albany—the oldest European settlement in the state.

RIGHT: Woodbridge Mansion in Perth's northern suburb of Guildford, was built in 1885 by the eminent Charles Harper, politician, explorer and publisher. One of Perth's grand old houses, the elegant two-storeyed rose-brick Victorian mansion is now owned by the National Trust.

TOP: Rottnest Island, 18 kilometres west of Fremantle, is Perth's favourite holiday destination. First settled in 1830, the island has had an interesting history, first as a prison, then for coastal defence and later as a holiday residence for the state Governors.

ABOVE: The STS *Leeuwin II* is a replica of a 19th century sailing ship berthed in Fremantle. Built in 1985, the ship is similar to those used by early explorers.

RIGHT: To West Australians, watersports are a way of life. In 1983, Australia claimed sailing's greatest prize—the America's Cup—and the victory celebrations were extensive.

ABOVE LEFT: St Francis Xavier Cathedral in Geraldton was designed and built by legendary priest Monsignor John Hawes, who left a legacy of churches in the diocese. Begun in 1916, and completed in 1938, the building features a combination of Byzantine and Romanesque architectural styles.

ABOVE RIGHT: The once thriving settlement of Greenough was built in the early 1860s, when it was the centre of a wheat growing area. Now the area is known for its leaning trees, Eucalypts that have bowed into precarious shapes as a result of the saltly sea winds weakening their limbs.

BELOW: The area around Mount Barker is a significant wine growing area, producing a range of excellent wines. Western Australia is increasingly becoming renowned for the quality of its viticulture, with areas such as Margaret River in particular finding a firm niche in the market.

ABOVE: The rugged cliffs of the Murchison River Gorge are the result of millions of years of weathering that has revealed layers of red rock. In the heart of wildflower country, the landscape takes on paintbox hues when the many varieties of flowers are in bloom.

LEFT: Like sentinels in the sand, the wind-carved limestone pinnacles of the Nambung National Park were formed thousands of years ago from shell deposits left behind when the sea receded. Their amazing shapes emerge from the sand dunes near Cervantes.

ABOVE: Connemara thoroughbred horses, standing on a purple carpet of Salvation Jane wildflowers, enliven the heart of the Avon Valley, north-east of Perth. The area is known as the haunt of 19th century bushranger Moondyne Joe, who used the Darling Range as his hideout.

LEFT: The flamboyant York town hall, built in 1911, features stucco pillars, balustrades and an elaborate corner pediment supporting a clock tower. Western Australia's most historic inland town, York was first settled in 1831, soon after the Swan River Colony.

OPPOSITE: Multicoloured walls of sandstone frame the spectacular Murchison River Gorge in the Kalbarri National Park.The amazing rock formations are even more colourful when the wildflowers burst into life.

ABOVE: The old State Hotel at Gwalia is a reminder of the prosperous days when a large underground gold mine made this a thriving centre, and the town boasted the first electric trams in Western Australia. Today the hotel houses the local museum and offices for the Sons of Gwalia mining company that operates a large open cut mine on the outskirts of town.

LEFT: Kalgoorlie–Boulder is one of the most important mining areas in Australia. Since prospectors found gold there in 1893, it has became one of the richest square miles on earth, dubbed the Golden Mile. This isolated and independent frontier town has been through boom and bust, and has a colourful history. Hannan's North Historic Mining Reserve (left) is one of the tourist mines where visitors can experience life as it was at the diggings more than 100 years ago.

ABOVE: The Stirling Park Range, rising steeply from the southern tableland, is a spectacular destination for bush walkers and one of Western Australia's outstanding botanical reserves. More than 1500 wildflower species grow here, including rare varieties found nowhere else. Bird life abounds, including parrots and honeyeaters.

LEFT: Sugarloaf Rock is located at the tip of Cape Naturaliste in the south-west of the state, where vast stretches of rugged coastline, stands of Karri trees and an amazing complex of caves can be found. The area is enclosed in the Leeuwin Naturaliste National Park, which winds past the picturesque Margaret River vine-growing area to Cape Leeuwin, where the Indian and Southern oceans meet.

BOTTOM LEFT: Bird life is prolific in the quiet majesty of dappled Karri forest in the Porongurup National Park, in the south-west corner of Western Australia. In spring, wildflowers carpet the landscape amid the ancient towering trees.

ABOVE: Smooth, eroded granite peaks jut unexpectedly from bush-clad coastline at Cheyne Bay, in Waychinicup National Park. The peaks are a continuation of the Many-Peaks Range. The spectacular coastal scenery offers expansive vistas of the Southern Ocean.

RIGHT: Werburgh's Chapel, 12 kilometres west of Mount Barker, was built between 1872 and 1873 and is preserved as a delightful example of pioneering dedication. Wrought iron was hand beaten on the property for the altar rail and chancel screen.

ABOVE: The Sydney–Perth train known as the Indian Pacific slices across the scorched landscape of the Nullarbor Plain. The world's longest straight track, it traverses 479 kilometres of desert and flat limestone tablelands of barren, treeless landscapes.

ABOVE RIGHT: The famous Wave Rock at Hyden, so-called for its resemblance to a massive wave, is one of Western Australia's best known natural formations. More than 2700 million years old, the 15-metre wall of granite has an unusual striped surface caused by chemical reactions and algae.

RIGHT: On the desolate sands of the Nullarbor Plain, near the border with South Australia, is the tiny outpost of Eucla, where a telegraph station was built in 1899 to link Perth and Adelaide. The ruins of the station can sometimes be seen protruding from the corrugated surface of the shifting sand dunes.

BELOW: Soft flowers of purple Mulla-mulla create a contrasting carpet for the world's largest rock—the impressive Burringurrah (Mount Augustus). An isolated monocline, the massive mound is eight kilometres long, and towers 730 metres above the plain of the Mount Augustus National Park. A billion years older than Uluru and twice the size, it is sacred to the local Aboriginals who have recorded their stories in art works on sites around the rock.

ABOVE: The earth's oldest and largest living fossils, stromatolites, flourish in the shallow waters of Hamelin Pool at Shark Bay Marine Park. The marine reserve is also home to dugongs, dolphins, sea turtles, sharks and whales and several species of seagrass.

LEFT: In an endless vista of a formidable landscape, sand dunes stretch as far as the eye can see near the junction of the Gascoyne and Lyons rivers, to the west of Carnarvon.

ABOVE: The rainbow coloured rocks of the ancient Hamersley Range are rich in iron ore. The heart of the mining region of the Pilbara, this rugged landscape is one of the oldest in Australia, dating back 3500 million years. The primitive grandeur of the rock encompasses waterfalls, vast gorges and spectacular peaks.

RIGHT: Iron ore has transformed Port Hedland into the largest deep-water port in Australia. A gigantic bucket wheel loads iron ore at the port.

ABOVE: In a glistening clear topaz sea, the sands of the isolated and remote Sisters Islands, in the Buccaneer Archipelago, emerge from the waters off the coast of the western Kimberley, north of Derby.

RIGHT: Pearls are farmed along the coast around Broome and the mission church at Beagle Bay has a pearl shell altar. The inlet north of Broome was named after the HMS *Beagle*, the ship from which it was surveyed in 1838.

ABOVE LEFT: Ferns flourish on the rugged walls of Emma Gorge on the million-acre cattle station El Questro. In this scenic region of the eastern Kimberley, waterfalls cascade from ancient escarpments and wide rivers cut through towering ranges.

ABOVE RIGHT: The last rays of the setting sun glow on one of the majestic peaks of the Cockburn Range in the east Kimberley, near Wyndham, the northernmost port in Western Australia.

RIGHT: When a meteorite hit the earth one or two million years ago, it left an almost perfectly circular crater in the desert at Wolfe Creek. Measuring 800 metres across and 50 metres deep, this amazing natural phenomenon is the second largest meteorite crater in the world.

BELOW LEFT: Aboriginal stockmen work the paddocks at Rose's Well Creek on Springvale Station, about 60 kilometres east of Hall's Creek.

BELOW RIGHT: Sporadic shafts of sunlight create light patterns on the flood plain as the King River, near Wyndham, curves sinuously to the Timor Sea. Wyndham is surrounded by spectacular tropical wetlands and rugged river gorges.

ABOVE: The distinctive striped sandstone rock of the Bungle Bungle Range in the Purnululu National Park has been weathered over 360 million years into rounded, beehive-shaped domes. Deep gorges intersect the massive rock towers of this imposing natural formation.

BELOW: Memories of a bustling gold town are recalled at Halls Creek, the site of Western Australia's first gold rush in 1885. Once a thriving centre of a thousand prospectors, the town is long abandoned and reduced to crumbling ruins of mud-brick buildings and a small cemetery.

ABOVE: Black Swans, which famously inhabit Perth's Swan River, are elegant nesting waterbirds that are widespread in Western Australia.

LEFT: The Kangaroo Paw is the floral emblem of Western Australia, and is found in swampy areas.

BELOW LEFT: The Saltwater Crocodile is one of Australia's two species of crocodile, and is responsible for occasional attacks on the unwary.

BELOW MIDDLE: The Drumhead Blackboy flowers in areas where bushfires have occured and is widespread in south-western areas of the state.

BELOW RIGHT: Dolphins are playful, sociable creatures, who enjoy following in the wake of a vessel. They often frequent sheltered harbours.

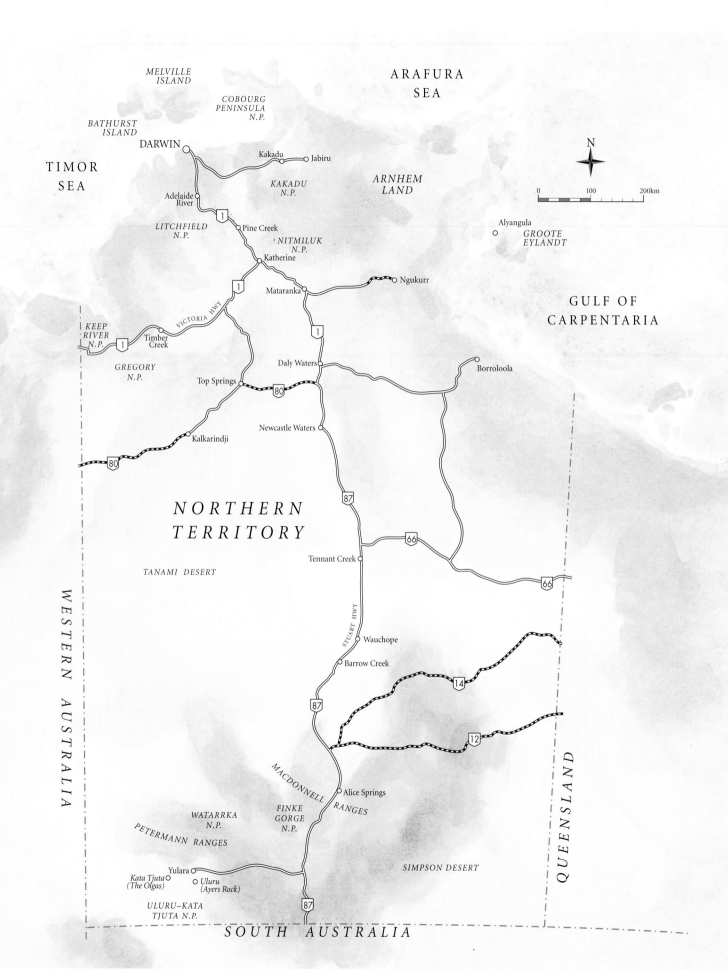

MELVILLE
ISLAND

COBOURG
PENINSULA
N.P.

ARAFURA
SEA

N

BATHURST
ISLAND

DARWIN

Kakadu   Jabiru

TIMOR
SEA

0   100   200km

Adelaide
River

KAKADU
N.P.

ARNHEM
LAND

1

LITCHFIELD
N.P.

Pine Creek

NITMILUK
N.P.

Alyangula

GROOTE
EYLANDT

Katherine

1

Mataranka   Ngukurr

GULF OF
CARPENTARIA

KEEP
RIVER
N.P.

1   Timber
Creek

VICTORIA HWY

1

Daly Waters   Borroloola

GREGORY
N.P.

Top Springs   80

Kalkarindji   Newcastle Waters

80

NORTHERN
TERRITORY

87

66

TANAMI DESERT

Tennant Creek

66

STUART HWY

Wauchope

Barrow Creek

14

87

WESTERN AUSTRALIA

12

MACDONNELL RANGES

Alice Springs

WATARRKA
N.P.

FINKE
GORGE
N.P.

PETERMANN RANGES

SIMPSON DESERT

QUEENSLAND

Yulara

Kata Tjuta
(The Olgas)   Uluru
(Ayers Rock)

ULURU–KATA
TJUTA N.P.

87

SOUTH AUSTRALIA

Northern Territory

The Northern Territory lies at the heart of Australia, a state of untamed landscapes steeped in legend and home to the Aboriginal people for more than 60 000 years. Its scorched red centre, permeated with the glowing hues of desert and rock, guards the secrets of the eons in an enigmatic panorama of infinite skies and sun-baked earth.

The capital of the Northern Territory, Darwin, was finally established as a trading post for the British Empire in 1869, after four aborted attempts due to the remoteness of the area and the inhospitable terrain. Although today's population of 70 000 still live with the constraints of year-round heat and geographical isolation, the buildings of the modern town are technologically advanced to defy the environment, and as such the city is cosmopolitan and lively. Darwin's modern streetscapes owe their presence to the fact that the city has twice been rebuilt, due to the ravages of wartime bombing in 1942 and the almost total destruction of the city by Cyclone Tracy on Christmas Day, 1974.

Not far from Darwin are two of Australia's most well-known natural reserves—Litchfield and Kakadu national parks.

Litchfield, to the south-west, is characterised by gushing waterfalls spilling over weathered sandstone escarpments and magnetic termite mounds, often more numerous than the trees. Kakadu, to the east, is a lush green wilderness area of spectacular beauty, and of World Heritage importance for its environmental diversity. Tropical rainforests merge with wetlands teeming with wildlife and waterfalls cascade into scenic rivers and billabongs. Here, too, primeval Aboriginal rock drawings have survived centuries of weathering as a proud record of the land's ancient people.

South of the Territory's tropical Top End, where life is governed by wet monsoons from November to March and complete dryness for the rest of the year, is the sun-baked red centre. Here, like the pulsating heart of the nation, is Uluru (Ayers Rock), recognised as Australia's most famous natural feature and the world's largest monolith, measuring 9 kilometres around the base and ascending 348 metres above the surrounding mulga plains to trick the eye with the light of the rising and setting sun. Of deep significance to the local

ABOVE: The dramatic silhouette of Uluru rises above the surrounding mulga plain in an awesome spectacle of majestic beauty. Once part of an ancient mountain range, the granite monolith at Australia's geographical heart is the country's most famous natural icon and a spiritual place of the Anangu Aboriginal people.

Aboriginal people, Uluru and the megaliths of Kata Tjuta (the Olgas) are riddled with fissures, caves and ravines, each with a spiritual association. The entire national park is included on the World Heritage list for its cultural and natural importance.

The Territory's transportation lifeline is the 1700 kilometre Stuart Highway, a sealed road that traces the route of the early explorers as they challenged the desolation of the centre on the way north. Water-starved ghost gums stand lonely sentinels in the barren outback desert that stretches to the quartzite peaks and ridges of the MacDonnell Ranges, riven by gorges and split by unrelenting extremes of temperature.

Many Australian's regard the Northern Territory as the nation's spiritual home. It is a land that reveals the symbols and stories of ancient Aboriginal tradition, etched on remote rocks and permeated with the fiery hues of desert and rock. More recently, legends of the pioneers of the Territory have grown to folklore status, recounting tales of men such as Flynn of the Inland (Rev. John Flynn) who established the Inland Mission, the Royal Flying Doctor Service and the Outback radio; John McDouall Stuart who crossed the continent from south to north; and Harry Lasseter, gold explorer. Like the terrain of the Northern Territory, their stories are of hardship and endurance, challenge and achievement. Territorians are proud of their heritage, their untamed province and the tough, pioneering spirit which conquered it.

LEFT: Darwin, the capital of the Northern Territory, is the only major city in northern Australia. Among lush tropical gardens and colourful open spaces, rise the modern buildings of a city which was almost entirely rebuilt after the devastation of Cyclone Tracy in 1974.

ABOVE: Darwin is renowned for its spectacular sunsets, but its gentle sunrises are equally pictures- que. Here, at Frances Bay, sillhouetted yachts at sunrise make this tranquil spot a popular place for early morning strolls.

RIGHT: Cruise ships, such as the *Marco Polo*, depart from Darwin Harbour, and tour boats take visitors on trips around the vast body of crocodile- infested water.

ABOVE: Government House has been known previously as the Residency and the House of Seven Gables. Built in classic colonial style between 1870 and 1879, it is a sprawling white building that sits in a tropical, palm-shaded garden overlooking the harbour. Its solid construction ensured it survived the ravages of Cyclone Tracy.

LEFT: Darwin's Parliament Building is the administrative hub of the Northern Territory. Previously governed by New South Wales, and latterly South Australia, the Northern Territory has been self-governing since 1978.

BOTTOM LEFT: Brown's Mart is one of the few remaining buildings in Darwin with a history, and is in fact the oldest surviving structure. Built in 1885 by an early trader and mayor named Brown, the building has had several uses, and has been extensively rebuilt after damage in several cyclones.

ABOVE LEFT: In the world-famous wilderness of Kakadu National Park, Twin Falls presents a glistening spectacle as it rushes through a towering gorge, which can only be reached during the summer months by canoe. Majestic waterfalls such as this tumble from steep escarpments as the South Alligator River flows through the park to the sea.

ABOVE RIGHT: The Nourlangie Gallery, at the Burrungguy art site, carries a huge mural of ceremonial figures which relate to the legend of the Lightening Dreaming. Sites of Aboriginal occupation in the area are believed to be over 20 000 years old.

RIGHT: Victoria River Downs, south of Timber Creek, is a cattle station par excellence. Stretching across some 4142 square kilometres, the station boasts a fleet of helicopters, used to muster over 35 000 head of cattle, and employs 21 people

ABOVE LEFT: Wangi Falls in Litchfield National Park issue from the plateau of the Tabletop Range. Easily accessible, these are the park's most popular falls, with a large pool and shaded lawns. The natural pool at the base was once a sacred fertility site to Aboriginal women, and forbidden to men.

ABOVE RIGHT: Jim Jim Falls is probably the most well-known water feature of the Northern Territory. Thousands of visitors flock to the area each year to witness the torrent of water as it drops 200 metres to the valley floor.

BELOW LEFT: Yellow Waters is a land-locked billabong, formed by Jim Jim Creek flowing into the floodplains near Coorinda. Popular cruise boat tours along the lushly vegetated waterways introduce visitors to the wildlife which inhabits this inland lagoon.

BELOW RIGHT: Herds of feral buffalo roam the Northern Territory. Bred to pest proportions, their numbers have been drastically reduced by culling. Here they are being captured for export.

THIS PAGE: To the west of Timber Creek, near the border with Western Australia, lies Keep River National Park. Its sandstone ridges, rocky escarpments and gorges are accessible and easily explored. The walk around the 4-kilometre Keep River Gorge takes in not only the local wildlife, but also ancient Aboriginal art sites (below) and giant boab trees (right).

ABOVE: One of the Northern Territory's most breathtaking landscapes is Katherine Gorge, a series of 13 canyons which winds back to the Arnhem Land plateau over a distance of 12 kilometres. The gorge is rich in animal and plant life, and glows bright when bathed in sunlight.

LEFT: Giant termite mounds exist all over the Northern Territory. Besides changing the face of the landscape, they are in fact cleverly-designed ventilation systems, protecting the termite colony from fluctuating temperatures.

BELOW: The settlement of Mataranka, near Katherine, is best known for its aqua-blue thermal pool, which nestles beneath tall palms in a four-hectare pocket of tropical forest in Elsey National Park. With an average water temperature of 34°C, the pool is a welcome retreat in this hot, dry region.

ABOVE LEFT: Rugged and independent, a cattleman and his horse mounting the crest of a hill may be a quintessential Outback scene, but it is also a reminder that horses are still very much working animals on the cattle and sheep stations of the Outback. Capable of traversing inhospitable terrain, they are depended upon to access remote locations and to muster livestock.

ABOVE RIGHT: The rock escarpments of Gulf country change with every bend, and among the most impressive of these are the formations known as the Hidden City, which date back over a billion years and are found on Nathan River Station near the Gulf of Carpentaria.

RIGHT: At the junction of the Tablelands and Carpentaria highways, not far from the Gulf of Carpentaria, sits the lonely Heartbreak Hotel. When travelling through the Territory along an isolated stretch of road, a roadhouse like this provides a welcome chance for a cool beer and a chat with the locals.

TOP: There is nothing else quite like the Devils Marbles, 114 kilometres south of Tennant Creek. Measuring up to six metres across, these huge granite boulders lie scattered in clusters around a shallow valley in the desert. While scientists say they are the result of a granite mass that broke up 2000 million years ago, the local Aboriginal people believe they are the eggs of the mythological Rainbow Serpent.

ABOVE LEFT: The Barrow Creek Telegraph Station, built in 1872, is one of only three remaining telegraph stations in the Territory. The tiny settlement on the Stuart Highway was named in 1860 after J.H. Barrow, a member of the South Australian parliament.

ABOVE RIGHT: Bred to survive the harsh conditions of the arid desert, camels were used by 19th century explorers as 'ships of the desert'—a vital means of transporting goods across vast distances. Today, various camel farms conduct tours along the dry bed of the Todd River in Alice Springs.

ABOVE: Alice Springs, the traditional home of the Arrerente Aboriginal people, is without doubt the most famous of the Outback towns. An oasis in the desert, it is now a modern, cosmopolitan centre, and a far cry from the dusty town immortalised by Nevil Shute in his novel *A Town Like Alice*. Surrounded by attractions ranging from desert parks to camel farms, 'The Alice' is a pocket of civilisation in the midst of an inhospitable land.

BELOW: Every year in October, visitors flock to Alice Springs to witness the world-famous Henley-on-Todd Regatta. This is a boat race with a twist—the vessels are propelled not by water, but by the competitors' feet racing along the dry and dusty bed of the Todd River.

LEFT: Australia's most famous Aboriginal artist, Albert Namatjira, is buried in the Alice Springs Memorial Cemetry in a simple grave. The painting that adorns his headstone is typical of his richly coloured landscapes, unmistakably capturing the essence and rare poetry of his ancestral land.

BELOW: The Telegraph Station at Alice Springs, now an historical reserve, was founded in 1871, as a vital link in the overland telegraph line between Adelaide and Darwin. Its contribution to the development of the Outback was enormous, reducing the isolation of the settlers and providing a means of communication with the outside world.

ABOVE: Deep in the heart of the magnificent red sandhills of the Ooraminna Ranges lies Ooraminna Bush Camp, located on the Deepwell cattle station. Besides offering visitors an authentic Australian Outback experience, the camp also houses a reconstructed police house and lock-up, used as a film set for *The Drover's Boy*.

BELOW: Tall, red walls of rock shade the sandy river bed which meanders through the narrow cleft known as Simpsons Gap. Majestic River Red and Ghost gums wind their way to a waterhole at the narrowest point, and agile Rock Wallabies inhabit the rockfall and nearby maze-like ridges.

ABOVE: The circular pound known as Gosse's Bluff that rises in the middle of the desert is the result of a force from outer space. Although various theories have been put forward as to its origin, geologists now agree that it was caused by the impact of a massive comet over 100 million years ago.

LEFT: Aboriginal people have lived in Australia for thousands of years, long before white man set foot on the shores of this vast continent. Theirs is a strong and complex culture, which asserts itself through ritual and art, and through increasingly vocal demands for the return of their traditional lands to Aboriginal custodianship.

ABOVE: When rain falls on a vast area of bare sand in central Australia, one of the plants that blazes with colour is the Parakeelya. Its colours range from white to purple, and Aboriginal people use the fleshy leaves for food.

RIGHT AND OPPOSITE BOTTOM: Watarrka National Park incorporates one of the most famous and spectacular sights of the Red Centre—Kings Canyon. Atop the steep, red walls of the gorge is a sparsely vegetated plateau, and the strange weathered formations known as the Lost City. In contrast to this starkly arid landscape is the lush valley known as the Garden of Eden, where native plants and trees grow in the shade of the canyon around the edge of a large waterhole.

ABOVE: Mount Giles, at 1283 metres above sea level, is the highest point of Ormiston Pound, a rocky amphitheatre which opens out at the end of the twisting Ormiston Gorge in the MacDonnell Ranges. Home to Kestrels and other birds of prey, both the gorge and pound are enclosed in an area of national park.

ABOVE: Palm Valley, in the Finke Gorge National Park, is a freak of nature. Prehistoric cycads cling to existence near small pools and wet sand, having survived here for over 10 000 years, along with ancient red cabbage palms—the only ones in the world. High above the palm trees, some of which are over 20 metres tall, tower the sandstone cliffs of the valley, an offshoot of Finke Gorge.

RIGHT: The vast dunes, in fact the longest in the world, of the Simpson Desert sweep across much of central Australia. Running north–south in unbroken stretches of over 100 kilometres, in the direction of the prevailing winds, the dunes are stable sand features that accumulated over millions of years.

LEFT: Visible from far across the desert, the sandstone monolith known as Chambers Pillar stands 30 metres tall on a 20-metre high pile of rubble. Used as a navigational tool by early explorers trekking across the desert from Adelaide to Alice Springs, it is estimated to be about 350 million years old. In Aboriginal legend, the pillar represents a banished Gecko ancestor.

BELOW: Glen Helen Gorge in the MacDonnell Ranges is the site of these craggy vertical ridges leading down the rock face, known as the Organ Pipes. A steep path leads over the gorge, to a viewpoint taking in the Finke Valley below and its neighbouring peaks beyond.

ABOVE: Twenty kilometres north of Uluru is the small township of Yulara, which crouches in the desert like a small insect lurking in the shadow of a mighty lizard. Sensitively designed to blend in with the duned desert landscape, the settlement incorporates a primary school as well as the Yulara Resort, which provides accommodation 'with a view'.

OPPOSITE: Kata Tjuta (the Olgas) is spiritually and geologically linked to Uluru. Consisting of a jumble of 36 massive domed megaliths, thought to be of a similar age to Uluru, it has great spiritual significance to the Anangu people. Kata Tjuta is rich in flora and fauna, with many species of wildflowers creeping over the craggy ridges of its mesmerising landscape.

ABOVE: At sunrise, after the first light has lifted the mantle of grey that descends nightly, Uluru gradually changes colour, from a series of magnificent deep, dark reds to a glow the colour of hot coals as the sun rises higher in the sky. To witness this awesome performance is a classic Australian experience, when one can almost feel the spirit ancestors of the Dreamtime passing by.

BELOW: The accommodation within the Ayers Rock Resort, at Yulara, ranges from camping grounds to the luxurious Sails in the Desert Hotel. Providing much needed shade is the distinctive canopy of white sails that gave the hotel its name, and which adds a sense of futuristic flair to the ancient red landscape.

ABOVE LEFT: The Dingo, an animal similar to the domestic dog, was introduced from Asia about 5000 to 8000 years ago. They hunt alone or in small packs.

ABOVE RIGHT: The Red Lotus flower is a vigorous, aquatic plant which flowers in winter.

BELOW LEFT: The Jacana is found on the Kakadu floodplains, and is uniquely equipped with long, straight claws for walking on floating vegetation.

BELOW MIDDLE: Sturt's Desert Rose is the floral emblem of the Northern Territory, and is found in gorges and gullies all over Australia.

BELOW RIGHT: Despite its appearance, the Thorny Devil is a slow-moving, harmless reptile.

THURSDAY
ISLAND

GULF OF
CARPENTARIA

MORNINGTON
ISLAND

CAPE YORK
PENINSULA

CORAL
SEA

GREAT BARRIER REEF

SOUTH
PACIFIC
OCEAN

Weipa

Cooktown

Daintree

Cairns

Atherton

1

HINCHINBROOK
ISLAND

Normanton

Ingham

1

83

LAWN HILL
N.P.

Townsville

WHITSUNDAY GROUP

NORTHERN TERRITORY

FLINDERS HWY

Charters
Towers

78

GREAT

Airlie Beach

Mt Isa

Cloncurry

66

DIVIDING

Mackay

83

RANGE

1

BRUCE HWY

Winton

Rockhampton

Boulia

66

Barcaldine

Emerald

66

Gladstone

Longreach

55

Biloela

BIRDSVILLE TRACK

71

CARNARVON
N.P.

1

Bundaberg

17

QUEENSLAND

Injune

Maryborough

FRASER
ISLAND

Gympie

Birdsville

Charleville

54

Noosa

SOUTH

Roma

Kingaroy

N

AUSTRALIA

BUNYA
MOUNTAINS
N.P.

54

BRISBANE

Toowoomba

Ipswich

Surfers Paradise

Cunnamulla

42

Goondiwindi

Gold Coast

0   100   200km

NEW SOUTH WALES

Queensland

Queensland, named the sunshine state for its near-perfect weather, is an immense kaleidoscope of lush, tropical rainforests, exotic beaches, pristine islands and, forming its vast interior, the scorched and barren lands of the great Outback.

The second-largest state in Australia, Queensland was put on the map in 1770 by Captain Cook. Officially founded in 1824, the state became independent from New South Wales in 1859. The northern settlements of the state are remote, and the vast distances from the capital, Brisbane, mean a definite divide between the tropical north and the cosmopolitan south.

Brisbane is Australia's third largest city, with 1.2 million residents living beside the Brisbane River as it flows into Moreton Bay. It is a busy and optimistic place, and visitors will find it hard to believe that it was once regarded as little more than a dull, provincial backwater.

The city's quintessential architecture, designed for the heat of the tropics, sees many of the houses elevated on stilts to take advantage of cooling breezes. Public buildings, too, are distinctive—the old Treasury Building is the best example of Italianate architecture in the Southern Hemisphere, and Parliament House was the first legislative building in the British Empire to be lit by electricity.

Bordering Brisbane's southern outskirts is the Gold Coast, with its 32 kilometres of white-sand surf beaches lined with multi-storey resorts. The focus of the Gold Coast is beachside Surfers Paradise. Queensland's beaches are internationally known as famous holiday destinations, and further north the beaches of the Sunshine Coast merge into hinterland that is a panorama of fertile plantations of pineapples, bananas and paw paws. Aboriginal legend surrounds the origins of the ten peaks of the Glasshouse Mountains, thrusting up from the plains of the hinterland, and presenting a craggy, ever-changing vista.

Lying off the coast is Fraser Island, the world's largest sand island and a World Heritage area. Dunes weathered into unusual towering formations fringe ancient rainforest, crystal creeks and lakes of blue, green and brown. Platypus Bay, off the west coast, is a regular stop for migrating Humpback Whales.

ABOVE: The rugged grandeur of Queensland's Lake Moogerah, in the picturesque Fassifern Valley, is surrounded by fertile farmland and volcanic peaks. The lake is located in the Mount French and Mount Edwards national parks.

Stretching 2000 kilometres from Bundaberg to Cape York Peninsula, beneath the azure waters off the coast, is the extraordinary Great Barrier Reef, World Heritage-listed as the world's most diverse ecosystem. Created over millions of years by the build-up of skeletons of coral polyps, the reef is home to an exotic underwater world of thousands of fish in radiant hues, darting around a seascape of flourishing coral, sponges and other colourful sea creatures.

Cairns is Queensland's most northerly city, gateway to the Atherton Tablelands and the dense rainforests of Cape York. This unchallenged wilderness is teeming with wildlife, ranging from dangerous crocodiles to enormous butterflies. Tully, south of Cairns, is the wettest place in Australia, with a rainfall of more than 4400 millimetres—ideal for growing sugar cane. Canefields lie in intricate patterns around Bundaberg, a place famous for not only its sugar production, but also its rum.

Queensland's remote Outback, on the fringe of the sand dunes of the Simpson Desert, is a region of legends, where the climate—either very wet or very dry—is all-powerful. The population of the Outback resides on vast cattle-stations, or in tiny settlements and small towns, such as Winton, renowned as the birthplace of both Australia's famous song *Waltzing Matilda* and Australia's national airline, Qantas (Queensland and Northern Territory Air Service); and barren Birdsville, with one pub and a store, famed for its 486-kilometre track and an annual horse race meeting.

Queensland is truly a state of extremes, a place rich in contradictions, from its exotic beaches and holiday resorts, to its unchallenged wilderness and dust-parched Outback. The southern towns and holiday areas are thriving and cosmopolitan, while the islands and towns of the north evoke the romantic splendour of the tropics.

LEFT: Brisbane is Queensland's cosmopolitan capital, sparkling in sunshine by day and with myriad lights reflecting on the river by night. The central business district looms across the Brisbane River, with the Captain Cook Bridge in the foreground and the Story Bridge in the background.

ABOVE: Brisbane's Riverside Centre comes alive on Sundays with a craft market and continuous entertainment. Ferries run across the river to the South Bank leisure precinct.

RIGHT: The Story Bridge is an essential link from the west of the city, and is Brisbane's equivalent of Sydney's Harbour Bridge. As such it looms large in the minds of residents as well as in its physical dimensions. Due to Brisbane's sandy soil, the bridge has some of the deepest foundations in Australia, reaching over 40 metres below the surface.

ABOVE: Brisbane city takes advantage of its riverside location. High rise towers offer panoramic views over the river with ferries and pleasure craft moored just steps from the central business district.

LEFT: A shaded colonnade of covered walkways surrounds the Great Court at the centre of the University of Queensland, St Lucia. Sculptor John Muller spent 14 years carving the sandstone pillars which feature coats of arms, and sculptures of faces and animals.

ABOVE: Queensland's Gold Coast is synonymous with three things—sun, sea and surf. With its plethora of top-quality hotels and resorts, and year-round good weather, many Australians make this sun-drenched stretch of coast their annual holiday destination. Currumbin is typical of all Gold Coast towns, with its magnificent beachfront and attractive bushland backdrop.

LEFT: The heart of the Gold Coast is the aptly named Surfers Paradise, a lively area renowned for its shopping centres, restaurants, bars and nightclubs. The high-rises are built along an endless stretch of golden beach, washed by the sparkling blue waters of the Pacific Ocean.

BOTTOM LEFT: The surf beaches of the Gold Coast are famous to boardriders the world over. Along the entire stretch of coast, perfect breaks can frequently be found.

ABOVE: The picturesque Noosa inlet on Queensland's Sunshine Coast has become a popular holiday destination. It has a superb setting at the mouth of the Noosa River, which winds from Lake Cooroibah into Laguna Bay. There is a Mediterranean atmosphere in Noosa's tree-lined streets, sidewalk cafés and boutique shopping.

LEFT: Shrouded with haze as the sun sets, the Glasshouse Mountains north of Brisbane in Queensland's Sunshine Coast hinterland were named by Captain Cook in 1770. The three volcanic plugs jut out of the coastal plain and each one is surrounded by national park to protect rare plant species and animals.

ABOVE: The Queensland coast from Bowen to Sarina is known as the Sugar Coast, where endless sugar cane plantations stretch as far as the eye can see. Almost 95 per cent of Australia's sugar production comes from Queensland, and the industry underpins the economic prosperity of many small communities.

RIGHT: During the cutting season, mechanical cane cutters are used to harvest the cane, replacing the old, arduous method of cutting by hand.

BOTTOM RIGHT: Thousands of hectares of crops are planted in Queensland for harvest each summer and winter, many of which are cereal grains. Wheat is the major winter crop, and much of it is exported for use in noodle production in Asia. The patterns formed in the agricultural lands west of Toowoomba are distinctive, and conform to the practice of contour farming.

TOP: Eroded by wind and rain, the Pinnacles are extraordinary coloured sand cliffs on Fraser Island, the largest natural sand island in the world. Covering 184 000 square kilometres, the landscape ranges from huge dunes to dense rainforest and freshwater lakes.

ABOVE: The traditional house known as the 'Queenslander' has a style and character that is uniquely Australian. Elevated on stilts to minimise heat and pests, most also feature an imaginative use of decorative detail.

LEFT: The historic town of Maryborough, on the Mary River, was a thriving township by 1861 as a result of the Gympie gold rush. The post office, built in 1869, is a remnant of this era, built in typical Victorian Classical Revival style, complete with an arcade and clock tower.

TOP: Between the mainland coast north of Mackay and the Great Barrier Reef are the Whitsundays, a group of 74 pristine islands with white sandy beaches and bush clad hills. Thousands of species of fish and hundreds of corals inhabit the waters around this marine park. Tidal sands and the sparkling azure waters of Whitehaven Beach on Whitsunday Island make this island in particular a pristine paradise.

ABOVE: Luxury Hayman Island is the most northerly of the Whitsunday Islands. An internationally acclaimed resort, it is accessible by launch, seaplane or helicopter.

RIGHT: Dunk Island is one of the most famous islands of the Great Barrier Reef. It is a tropical paradise which maintains a strict balance between the preservation of an exquisite natural habitat and the needs of the tourists that come to soak up the Queensland sun.

ABOVE: Turquoise waters surround Hardy Reef, one of the many reefs that form the Great Barrier Reef Marine Park, near Bowen and the Whitsunday Islands. Visitors can dive from the passenger launch *Reefworld* to enjoy a glimpse into an underwater wonderland.

LEFT: The Great Barrier Reef is over 2000 kilometres long and snorkelling is a popular way to explore the colourful world of coral and sea life that lives beneath the vividly blue waters.

ABOVE: Castle Hill towers above the elegant city of Townsville. Many heritage buildings date from 1865, when it was founded as a port for the north coast. High rise towers contrast with the colonial architecture on the banks of the Ross Creek.

LEFT: Rosebank, at Townsville, is a restored villa, dating from the late 19th century, and one of the few grand houses in North Queensland. Sweeping lawns and wide shady verandahs with elevated foundations are designed to minimise the heat of the tropical climate.

BOTTOM LEFT: Cairns, the most northerly city in Queensland, grew up around the mouth of Trinity Inlet. The city has long been associated with game fishing, and fishermen bring their marlin to be weighed at the marina.

LEFT: The graceful Victorian town of Charters Towers was built on the riches of gold mining, and residents were so proud of their community that they referred to it as 'the World'. Originally built as a shopping arcade in 1888, the Stock Exchange is an example of the elaborate architecture of the time, a combination of Italianate and Classical Revival styles.

BELOW LEFT AND RIGHT: Ravenswood, 130 kilometres inland from Townsville, was a thriving gold town between 1900 and 1912, rivalling Charters Towers with its prosperity. Now a virtual ghost town, it is testimony to the fluctuating fortunes of gold prospecting. The beer still flows, however, in the Imperial Hotel, a fine example of late Victorian architectural extravagance, where customers can still enter through the batwing doors.

ABOVE: Rainforest clads the slopes of Queensland's highest peak, Mount Bartle Frere, towering behind the heart of sugar cane country south of Cairns. The Russell River cuts through steep gorges, then winds its way to the coast through national park.

RIGHT: Wallaman Falls, located near Ingham in Lumholtz National Park, is Australia's longest single drop waterfall at 305 metres. A zig-zag path leads through tropical rainforest to the bottom of the falls.

OPPOSITE: Hinchinbrook Island, 30 kilometres off the coast north of Townsville, is the world's largest island national park. Old volcanic peaks are covered in a rainforest wilderness sheltering a wealth of wildlife. The Herbert is one of nine rivers that cascade over spectacular waterfalls on the way to sweeping sandy beaches and extensive mangrove swamps.

ABOVE: Cascading down a sheer rock face, the Millaa Millaa Falls descend into a crystal pool in the rainforest, sheltered by ferns and impatiens. Near the Palmerston National Park, the falls are on the escarpment of the Atherton Tablelands, the cool tropical region inland from the coast.

OPPOSITE: North of the Atherton Tablelands, in the Daintree National Park, the Mossman Gorge is home to some of Queensland's most beautiful tropical rainforest. Rare birds shelter in the overhanging green trees and fish inhabit the cool, shady pools.

ABOVE: In 1770, when Captain Cook stepped ashore at what is now Cooktown, he would have seen this view of Cape Bedford from the Grassy Hill Lookout. The lighthouse, built in England and shipped to Cooktown in 1885, was used for over 100 years and has been recently restored.

BELOW LEFT: Torres Strait Islanders live on the three-kilometre Thursday Island, the centre of the Torres Strait group, off the northern tip of the Cape York Peninsula.

BELOW RIGHT: Once an important port on the Gulf of Carpentaria, Normanton is best known for its railway station, built in 1891 and now listed by the National Trust. It is the starting point for the Gulflander, a train that links the town with Croydon.

TOP: World Heritage-listed Lawn Hill National Park is an oasis of tropical rainforest in the dry arid landscape of western Queensland. The Duwadarri waterhole, sheltering in a cool gorge, is fed by springs in the limestone plateau to the west. Pandanus palms, figs and pines abound, and the freshwater wildlife includes crocodiles, turtles and rare fish. There is evidence of human occupation here from 17 000 years ago.

ABOVE LEFT: Mt Isa, the mining town in Outback Queensland, claims to be the largest city in the world, sprawling over almost 41 000 kilometres. First mined for copper in the 1880s, it has vast deposits of zinc and is the world's biggest producer of silver and lead. The underground mine, which is open to visitors, is the largest in Australia.

ABOVE RIGHT: Boulia in Outback Queensland is the capital of the region known as Channel Country, first settled in 1876. The historic museum house is a repository for local memorabilia and the area abounds with legends of the eerie 'min min light', a ghostly phosphorescence.

TOP: Few places in Australia are as lonely or as isolated as the tiny settlement of Birdsville, which consists of little more than a pub and a few houses—except for a couple of days every year. On the first Saturday in September, the Birdsville Races are a highlight of the Outback social calendar. Visitors travel long distances to attend the event, held on a barren desert racetrack, and stay long enough to make sure all the beer is consumed.

ABOVE: Birdsville sits on the edge of the Simpson Desert, with Sturt Stony Desert to the south-east. The latter was named after Charles Sturt, the first European explorer to venture into this lonely area.

LEFT: A few blokes having a yarn outside a pub, while the desert sun sets in a blaze of colour, is a quintessentially Australian Outback scene. The population of 100 in Birdsville have little other entertainment than their local hotel, where the beer at least is cool and the welcome warm.

ABOVE LEFT: For most of the year, not much rain falls around Cooper Creek, but the monsoonal rains of the summer months swell the Barcoo and Thomson rivers, which meet at Cooper Creek. Water spills over onto the landscape, spreading out to fill gullies and forming intricate patterns which are most noticable from the air.

ABOVE RIGHT: At the centre of one of the state's most prosperous wool and beef areas is the town of Longreach, home of the Australian Stockman's Hall of Fame, and a popular tourist destination. The exhibition focuses on life in the bush, using a time line and the latest audio-visual techniques.

LEFT: Off the road to Innamincka is the Dig Tree, the famous final act of the Burke and Wills tragedy. William Brahe, in charge of the support party, buried food under the tree on 21 April, 1861 and carved the words 'Dig under 3ft W' on the trunk. It is an irony of history that the starving explorers returned to the camp only seven hours after Brahe abandoned hope of their return and left.

TOP AND ABOVE RIGHT: Carnarvon National Park forms part of the table-land of the Great Dividing Range, consisting of more than 25 000 hectares. Among the many outstanding natural features of the area are the strange formations known as the Chimneys, near Mount Moffat. The park is also home to more than 50 Aboriginal sites (above right).

ABOVE LEFT: The distances in Australia are vast, and many roads are lonely and isolated. The lack of petrol and food stops means good preparation is essential when undertaking a journey in the Outback.

RIGHT: Injune, north of Roma, is the southern gateway to the Carnarvon National Park and the hub of a pastoral and agricultural district in central southern Queensland. Cattle drovers have a lonely task, covering vast distances on horseback.

ABOVE: The Green Turtle is one of the many creatures that live on the Great Barrier Reef. Australia's most important turtle rookery is at Mon Repos Beach near Bundaberg.

LEFT: Sunflowers, originally from North America, are grown commercially in Queensland for their seeds and oil.

BELOW LEFT: Butterfly Cod are among the thousands of colourful and exotic fish found on the Great Barrier Reef.

BELOW MIDDLE: Queensland is renowned for its vividly coloured tree species, including the brilliant Poinciana.

BELOW RIGHT: The Wallaby, like the Kangaroo, is a pouched marsupial. It mostly inhabits open forest, woodland and grassland.

Acknowledgements

Firstly, I am endebted to Alison, my wife, for her encouragement, forbearance and the many hours contributed to this book. To those who have travelled with me from time-to-time, my gratitude: Don Donovan, Detlef Kramer, Richard Hoskins, Roger Nicoll and Hugh Smith particularly. Their patience and good humour were put to the test on a number of occasions.

My thanks are also due to the Landmark Parkroyal hotel; Victoria Racing Club; Terry Reece; Peter & Kaye Davidson; Nick Green; Bill & Jean Hayes, for their special cooperation; and to so many people, too numerous to mention individually, who have assisted at various times in some way.

Finally, my thanks to the team at New Holland with whom I have worked: Anouska Good, Sophie Church, Linda Maxwell, Pauline Kirton and Kirsti Wright.

PHOTOGRAPHIC NOTES

Minolta 35mm and Mamiya 6x7 cameras and lenses were used for most of the pictures in this book. However, some were taken on Linhof 4x5 and Leica cameras using Schneider lenses. Focal length of the lenses ranged from 20mm to 840mm. Most of the film was Fuji processed by Image Works.

ABOVE: A spiky Pandanus palm, sillhouetted against the deep red glow of an Australian sunset, is a classic beachside image.

Index

First published in Australia in 2000 by
New Holland Publishers (Australia) Pty Ltd
Sydney · Auckland · London · Cape Town

14 Aquatic Drive Frenchs Forest NSW 2086 Australia
218 Lake Road Northcote Auckland New Zealand
24 Nutford Place London W1H 6DQ United Kingdom
80 McKenzie Street Cape Town 8001 South Africa

National Library of Australia
Cataloguing-in-Publication Data:

Smith, Robin, 1927–.
Portrait of Australia

Includes index.
ISBN 1 86436 611 7.

1. Australia — Pictorial works. I. Title.

919.4

Publishing General Manager: Jane Hazell
Publisher: Averill Chase
Publishing Manager: Anouska Good
Project Editor: Sophie Church
Text: Sophie Church and Pauline Kirton
Designer: Linda Maxwell
Research: Kirsti Wright
Cartography: Colin Wynter Seton
Reproduction: Colourscan(Singapore)
Printer: Tien Wah Press

CAPTIONS

Page i: skull in the desert, Queensland; page ii: Porepunkah, Ovens Valley, Victoria;
page iii: Bunyeroo landscape, South Australia; page iv: poplar plantation, Murray valley, Victoria.